The Top 10 Guide to Rome™

By

Sharri Whiting

The Internationalist
96 Walter Street/Suite 200
Boston, MA 02131 USA

The Internationalist®

International Business, Investment and Travel

Published by:
The Internationalist Publishing Company
96 Walter Street/Suite 200
Boston, MA 02131, USA
Tel: 617-354-7722
Publisher@internationalist.com

ISBN 1-891382-20-9

Special Sales:
Books of the Internationalist Publishing Company are available for bulk
purchases at special discounts for sales promotions, corporate identity
programs or premiums. The Internationalist Publishing Company
publishes books on international business, investment and travel. For
further information contact the Special Sales department at: Special Sales,
The Internationalist, 96 Walter Street/Suite 200, Boston, MA 02131.

The Internationalist Publishing Company
96 Walter Street/Suite 200
Boston, MA 02131 USA
Tel: 617-354-7722
Sales@internationalist.com

e-mail: publisher@internationalist.com
web site: http://www.internationalist.com

Welcome to Rome.

From its legendary beginnings almost three thousand years ago, Rome grew to rule a vast empire. Today, it remains one of the greatest cities of the world. Powerful, dynamic, pulsating with life and history, Rome has been the inspiration of artists and writers for centuries. Here, the visitor is transported back in time and place to the days of emperors, gladiators and empire-building visionaries. Rome is a city where history is juxtaposed with modern design and innovation, where movie stars and housewives shop side by side in the ancient markets. There is more to see and do in just a few blocks of Rome than in most other leading cities of the world combined. What a disappointment it would be to visit Rome and not experience the very best the city has to offer.

THE TOP 10 GUIDE TO ROME is designed to help you experience the very best of Rome: the best restaurants, the best museums, the best sights and the best entertainment. THE TOP 10 GUIDE TO ROME is the only guide you will need. Turn the pages and let it lead you through the best of classic and contemporary Rome.

There is so much to Rome that you can get overwhelmed and miss some of the city's outstanding high points. Sharri Whiting makes sure you experience the city's crown jewels: the great museums, the dramatic panoramas, the romantic restaurants, and some of the world's most famous works of art.

Whether you are visiting for a few days or a few weeks, on a business trip or a once-in-a-lifetime vacation, THE TOP 10 GUIDE TO ROME lets you focus on the best of everything so that your Rome experience is a rich and rewarding one.

THE TOP 10 TRAVEL GUIDES are designed to meet the needs of today's sophisticated travelers. They highlight the best the world has to offer. They are available for other cities of the world. Just ask your bookseller.

Best wishes for an exciting visit to Rome.

Sharri Whiting

Sharri Whiting divides her time between Rome and Umbria in Italy and Boston, Ma. Few know Rome as well as Sharri. She has navigated the chaos of the Rome's wild traffic in her tiny Fiat 500 — while reading maps, changing gears, and avoiding darting pedestrians, mad taxi drivers and modern gladiators in four-wheeled chariots; and she has walked the hidden quiet streets of the ancient city, studying the indelible marks of over three thousand years of history. She has shopped, dined and experienced the best of Rome. Now she brings the Rome she knows so well to you. Whiting is married to an Italian diplomat (and a Roman), Piero DeMasi, under whose guidance she began to know Rome intimately. A former president of the American Women's Association of Rome, Whiting writes about Italy for newspapers, magazines and e-zines, and is a guest lecturer at the American University of Rome. Her knowledge of the city gives readers inside information about Rome and the Romans.

Contents

Rome

THE TOP 10 GUIDE

The Top 10 Must See Attractions of Rome

The Italians call her Roma and, just as the adage says, she definitely wasn't built in a day. In fact, the city is over 2,700 years old; a lady of timeless beauty whose glorious architecture and rich colors reflect the best of western civilization. Great poets and writers, such as Lord Byron, Keats, and Shelley believed that to be fully educated, a person should experience this magnificent city and be inspired by her.

Today, dynamic Roma is called the Eternal City, not because of her age, but because it seems like it would take an eternity to see all the wealth of art and culture she has accumulated over the centuries. Where to begin?

The list below is the place to start. It is the essential Rome, the very best of Rome. And remember, by tossing a coin into the Trevi Fountain you ensure your return to this exciting city.

1. The Colosseum

The Colosseum was commissioned in 72 AD by the Emperor Vespasian. Beyond the graceful, arched entrances, 55,000 spectators once watched gladiatorial contests and wild animal fights. The Colosseum's sun-bleached stones and soaring staircases, along with its grand history, make it the most majestic symbol of ancient Rome. Be sure to take your pictures outside with a costumed Roman Centurian, but settle the price first.
Piazza del Colosseo, open daily except for public holidays.

2. Sistine Chapel

The frescoes of the Vatican Museum's main chapel were created by Michelangelo, Perugino and Botticelli. Michelangelo's contribution, the ceiling, is arguably the greatest artwork on earth. Now that its colors have been restored to their original vibrant glory, the ceiling is more stunning than ever to view. The fastest route to the Sistine Chapel is a 1.5- hour walk from the main museum entrance through a labyrinth of spectacular collections. The Raphael rooms and the map gallery are particularly impressive. Don't let long waiting lines outside keep you away— the museum is huge and accommodates thousands of visitors each day.
Citta' del Vaticano (Vatican City), open daily except for religious and public holidays (there are many); free last Sunday of the month.

3. Spanish Steps

In the 17th century, the owners of the Trinita' dei Monti property decided to link the church to the Piazza di Spagna below with a grand staircase; thus was born one of the Rome's most distinctive and beautiful landmarks. On sunny days, the steps are crowded with tourists and students, relaxing and enjoying the free show in the piazza below. In the spring, the City of Rome decorates the steps with hundreds of pink azalea bushes.

Piazza di Spagna

4. Roman Forum

The center of political, commercial, and judicial life in ancient Rome, the Forum was home of, and witness to, pivotal moments in the grand history of the Roman Empire. The best view of these ruins is from behind the Campidoglio, particularly at sunset or on summer nights, when the Forum is lighted.

Pedestrian entrances to the Forum are on Largo Romolo e Remo and Via di San Gregorio, open daily except public holidays.

5. St. Peter's

The basilica of St. Peter is the center of the Roman Catholic faith to people all over the world. And, it is an impressive symbol of the city itself. Its 450-foot-high dome, the tallest on earth, was designed by Michelangelo. From the basilica's roof, visitors can view the Eternal city either as it spreads out in its pink and white glory or from the River Tiber snaking through the ancient neighborhoods. Inside the church are the tomb of St. Peter, the patron saint of Rome, and Michelangelo's exquisite marble sculpture, the Pieta.

Piazza San Pietro

6. Trevi Fountain

The star of some of the most romantic movies ever produced, the Trevi Fountain is a symbol of *amore* to tourists from all over the world. The massive fountain almost dwarfs the piazza in which it sits, but visitors don't seem to care - they're mesmerized by the clear waters that surge around Neptune and his Tritons. Packed with people almost 24 hours a day, this piazza is the site of rendevous and pick ups, photos and wishes. Remember that throwing a coin into this fountain assures your return to Rome.

Piazza di Trevi

7. The Catacombs

Visiting one of Rome's ancient underground catacombs is something you must do (unless you're claustrophobic). Though there are catacombs located throughout Rome, the most important cluster of is out along the Via Appia Antica, the Old Appian Way. Because so many saints were buried in these cool, dim tunnels, the various tombs later became shrines. One of the best catacomb tours is offered (in half a dozen languages) at the Catacombs on San Callisto. The Catacombs of San Sebastiano are nearby. Around the corner are the Catacombs of Domitilla, Rome's largest grouping, where some of the tombs date from the first century AD.

All are on or near the Via Appia Antica, near restaurants, cafes and other outdoor historic sites, such as the drum-shaped Tomb of Cecilia Metella.

Pieta

8. Piazza Navona

There is so much going on in this elongated, oval piazza that some consider it to be the real center of Rome. Formerly the Stadium of Diocletian, the piazza's focal point is Bernini's dramatic Fontana dei Fiumi. Piazza Navona is filled with outdoor restaurants, a collection of bars and cafes, artists, musicians, students, tourists, and "real" Romans who live in the neighborhoods.

Piazza Navona

9. The Pantheon

This two-thousand-year-old landmark, once a "temple to all the gods," is a marvel of engineering. Its structural plan, as well as its dome, were the inspiration—and blueprint—for the great domes of St. Peter's, the duomo in Florence, and the U.S. Capitol in Washington, D.C. The interior, lit by a single skylight 140 feet above the floor, is an awe-inspiring respite from the bustle of the piazza outside.

Piazza della Rotonda

10. The Borghese Museum

Re-opened in the late 1990s after extensive restoration, the museum is located in the Villa Borghese, at the center of the Borghese park. In the early 19th century, the entirety of the Borghese family's magnificent art collection was assembled in the villa. On exhibit are the famous Canova sculpture of Pauline Borghese; numerous spectacular Bernini works; the statue of Sleeping Hermaphrodite (150BC); and a marvelous collection of paintings. Reservations advised.

Piazzale Scipione Borghese, open daily

The Top 10 Museums of Rome

Over half of the world's great art can be found in Italy; much of it is housed in the myriad museums of Rome. Make it a point to see the collections in the sites listed below; they are a tribute to man's incredible artistic accomplishments throughout the centuries.

1. The Vatican Museums

Even without the magnificent Sistine Chapel or the Raphael Rooms, the Vatican Museums would still be remarkable. The shortest tour through its vast array of exhibits takes one-and-a-half hours, while the longest is five hours.
Citta' del Vaticano

2. The Borghese Museum

When the Borghese Museum re-opened in the late 1990s, it re-introduced the world to an array of Bernini sculptures, Caravaggio paintings, and the ornate décor of the Villa Borghese itself.
Piazzale Scipione Borghese 5

3. Capitoline Museums

The imposing bronze statue of Marcus Aurelius greets visitors to this site. Inside, the Palazzo Nuovo displays two floors of classical sculpture. Across the piazza, in the Palazzo dei Conservatori, are Caravaggio's "St. John the Baptist" and the famous Etruscan bronze "She-wolf," the creature who later became symbol of the city of Rome.
Piazza del Campidoglio

4. The Etruscan Museum

While inside the Villa Giulia, vistors will partake of the history of the enigmatic Etruscans. Exhibits include a reconstruction of an entire Etruscan temple.
Piazzale Villa Giulia 9

5. The Keats-Shelley Memorial House

Memorializes the lives of the English poets John Keats and Percy Bysshe Shelley, both of whom lived and died in Italy. Tribute is also paid to the Shelley women.
Piazza di Spagna 26

6. Palazzo Massimo alle Terme

Many of the collections belonging to the Museo Nazionale Romano are housed in the Palazzo Massimo alle Terme, including the archaeological section and the spectacular frescoes of Livia.
Piazza dei Cinquecento 68

7. Palazzo Venezia

One of the first Renaissance buildings constructed in Rome, the façade of the Palazzo Venezia Museum has, as its heart, the balcony of Mussolini. The dictator used the entirety of the structure as his headquarters. Inside is one of the world's finest collections of Renaissance art.
Via del Plebiscito 118

8. The Museo Nazionale Romano

Most of the antiquities that have been discovered in Rome since the last quarter of the 19th century have their permanent homes here. One of the leading museums of classical art.
In the Baths of Diocletian, Viale Enrico de Nicola 79

9. The Galleria Doria Pamphilj

Holds works by some of the greatest artists of the Renaissance, including: Titian, Caravaggio, Lotto and Guercino.
Piazza del Collegio Romano 1A

10. The Palazzo Altemps

This branch of the Museo Nazionale Romano holds part of the institution's impressive collection of classical, Greek and Roman art, includng sculpture.
Via Sant'Apollinare 8

The Top 10 Architectural Sites Of Rome

There is architecture and there is archeology. In Rome it is sometimes hard to differentiate them. If you are looking for outstanding Roman architecture, the following list will give you a good start. Don't be afraid to wander, however, as you will surely see fascinating buildings on every corner.

1. The Pantheon

One of the great spiritual buildings in the world, the open dome served as an inspiration to such figures as Brunelleschi and Michelangelo. It was designed by the Emperor Hadrian (118-125 AD) to replace an earlier temple built by Marcus Agrippa. The opening in the top of the rotunda provides the only light. The great artist Raphael is buried here, along with the Kings of Italy.
Piazza della Rotonda

2. The Piazza del Campidoglio

Designed by Michelangelo at the request of Pope Paul III, this piazza is thought to be the most perfect public space ever constructed. Michelangelo's paving pattern was so important to the design that it was laid in exactly as the original plan had demanded, even though it was done 400 years later. The piazza faces west, towards St. Peter's, which is Michelangelo's other great commissioned work.

3. St. Peter's Basilica

The most magnificent church in Christendom, St. Peter's rises above the Vatican Hill, crowned by Michelangelo's beautiful dome. The entrance to St. Peter's was vastly improved in the 1920's, when the crumbling, centuries-old houses were torn down to build the Via della Conciliazione, a broad street that leads into the Piazza San Pietro.
Piazza San Pietro

4. Palazzo Farnese

This most imposing 16th century palace is another of Michelangelo's masterpieces. Currently the site of the French Embassy in Rome, the palazzo is open to visitors one day a week by advance appointment. It is worth the advance planning to see the Carracci frescoes, which are said to rival the ceiling of the Sistine Chapel.
Piazza Farnese

5. Castel Sant' Angelo (Hadrian's Tomb).

Built by Emperor Hadrian in 128 AD as a mausoleum, the Castel Sant'Angelo is the imposing round fortress that sits along the Tiber River near the Vatican. Inside are dank dungeons, a military museum, and a café overlooking the city. On top stands a brooding statue of the Archangel Michael, from whom the castel takes its name. Serving as the residence of the pope in times of unrest, the Castel Sant' Angelo is connected to the Vatican by the Vatican Corridor, built in 1277 to provide an escape route for the Pontiff.

Lungotevere Castello

6. Piazza del Popolo.

The Piazza del Popolo was created by Valadier, the designer of the Pincio Gardens above. It was originally just a muddy field, but Valadier envisioned a beautiful piazza in its place and designed the gigantic earth-moving project necessary to achieve it. It is considered one of the most beautiful planned squares in the world. The obelisk in the center, over 3,000 years old, was brought to the city by Augustus to decorate the Circus Maximus after the conquest of Egypt.

7. Palazzo Barberini.

One of the great palaces of the Baroque period, the palazzo Barberini was built beginning in 1623 for Pope Urban VIII and his family. The original architect, Carlo Maderno, designed it as a country villa surrounded by gardens; he died in 1629 and Bernini assumed the job, with Borromini as his assistant. The most fabulous of the incredibly decorated rooms is the Gran Salone with its ceiling fresco by Pietro da Cortona. The palazzo houses part of the Galleria Nazionale d'Arte Antica, with works by Filippo Lippi, El Greco and Caravaggio.

Via della Quattro Fontane, 13.

8. Palazzo della Cancelleria.

A prime example of early Renaissance architecture, the building was begun in 1485, financed by gambling winnings of Cardinal Raffaele Riario. The Doric courtyard is decorated with roses, the emblem of the Riario family. The interior was redecorated after the Sack of Rome in 1527 with works by Giorgio Vasari, del Vaga, and Salviati. (Michelangelo was said to be unimpressed by the quality of Vasari's work).

Piazza della Cancelleria

9. American Academy in Rome

An ecclectic collection of buildings including the wonderful 17th century Villa Aurelia, the Taverna Rustica (an old tavern), the turn-of-the century Belacci, and the centerpiece, the palazzo designed by American architects McKim, Mead, and White in 1913. The gardens of the American Academy, especially the Bass Garden, are appreciated by landscape architects.
Via Angelo Masina 5.

10. Esposizione Universale di Roma (EUR).

Despite its connection with the despised fascist regime, the EUR complex (along with the Foro Italico and the United Nations Food and Agriculture building) best exemplifies the effect Mussolini had on the architecture and city planning of modern Rome. Located in the south of the city, the complex was originally built for a kind of world's fair to be held in 1942. The architecture, with its square and looming marble edifices, includes the Palazzo della Civilta' del Lavoro, called the "Square Colosseum." Finished in the 1950s and filled with government and private offices and residences, EUR has been a successful effort in city planning. The Museo della Civilta' Romana has a gigantic scale model of Rome at the time of Constantine.
Piazza G. Agnelli and surrounding areas.

Pantheon

The Top 10 Archeological Sites of Rome

1. Palatine Hill

Legend says that Romulus and Remus were brought up by a she-wolf in a cave on this very spot. After besting his brother in battle, Romulus founded the city of Rome. The Palatine is the site of 8th century BC Iron Age ruins. Also on site are later buildings, including the houses of the great orator Cicero, the poet Catullus, and Augustus and Livia. The ruins of the palace of Tiberius are here as well, along with those of Domitian's palace. Nearby is the Stadium of Domitian, which was used for foot races in the 6th century. Nero's Cryptoporticus runs beneath, a series of underground corridors that connect his golden house, the Domus Aurea, with the palaces of other emperors on the Palatine.

2. The Roman Forum (Foro Romano)

The center of life in ancient Rome, the Forum and the adjacent Trajan Market, are the most complicated of Roman archeological sites. While you can wander the ruins at will, it is important to take a map for a full understanding of the huge site.

3. Colosseum

The Colosseum may be the most impressive, individual monument in Rome. Certainly, it is the most recognizable. Up to fifty thousand spectators once sat in the incredible travertine marble stadium watching gladiators fight each other or hunt animals. Built in 79-80 AD, the Colosseum saw its last staged combats in the 5th and 6th centuries.

4. The Baths of Caracalla and Diocletian

Roman baths were social centers, where citizens spent long afternoons enjoying themselves. The Baths of Caracalla were finished in 217 AD and functioned for approximately 300 years. Their ruins are amazingly well preserved; standing walls and shards of mosaics indicate the uses of the rooms. The Baths of Diocletian had a capacity of 3000 bathers, while Caracalla accommodated 1500. Located near the Piazza della Republica, the best-preserved areas of these baths house the church of Santa Maria degli Angeli.

5. Circus Maximus

Once Rome's largest stadium, today it is a broad grassy plain. The stadium was built and expanded from the 4th century until 549 AD, when the last races were run. At its height, 250,000 fans cheered the chariot races and wild animal fights.

6. Via Appia Antica/Tomb of Cecilia Metella, 25BC

The Appian Way was built during the time of the Roman Republic. It is one of the great roads that kept communications, troops, and commerce moving throughout the massive territory. Today, along the three remaining miles of the old road, it is possible to see the original paving stones. The Old Appian Way is lined with catacombs, statuary, and the well-known Cecilia Metella.

7. The Stadium of Domitian, 92AD

Rome's beautiful Piazza Navona was first the site of Domitian's staduim. Athletic contests were held there, before crowds of 33,000. The stadium dates back to the 1st century, while the piazza's Baroque design was implemented in the 17th century. Legend says the piazza was flooded for mock naval battles.

8. Aurelian Wall

Much of the Aurelian Wall, begun by emperor Aurelian (270-5 AD), is still in place. Eleven miles around, with 18 gates and 381 towers, the wall took in all the seven hills of Rome. The best preserved gateway is the Porta San Sebastiano, which leads to the Via Appia Antica. The gatehouse is a museum, containing information about the history of the wall, which was Rome's main line of defense until 1870.

9. Catacombs

Of the catacombs located on the Appian Way, San Callisto and San Sebastiano are the best. San Callisto features group tours in several languages which take visitors into the 3rd century funeral chapel and the 5th century frescoes. The 17th century San Sebastiano church sits above the catacombs of the same name. The nearby Catacombs of Domitilla are the largest in Rome, with many tombs from the 1st and 2nd centuries having no Christian connection. The Via Latina catacomb, the "Ipogeo," is covered by perfectly preserved frescoes of the Old and New Testaments and is open by appointment only through the Vatican.
Tel 06 44 65 610.

10. Testaccio Hill

An artificial hill, Testaccio was used as a landfill in early Roman times, 140 BC to 250 AD. It was actually a dump for discarded amphoras used to carry goods to nearby warehouses. Rising over 100 feet, the "Hill of Potsherds" is now a grassy knoll and plans are underway to make it into a park.

The Top 10 Churches of Rome

Rome is the city of churches; 913 of them at last count. Magnificent works of architecture and design, they are filled with glorious art. Some of history's greatest artists created their masterpieces for Roman churches, on the orders of popes and princes. Women should cover shoulders; no shorts for men or women.

1. St. Peter's

St. Peter's attracts millions of visitors of all different faiths from all over the world. Viewing Michelangelo's dome and his soul satisfying sculpture, The Pieta is essential to the experience of visiting St. Peter's. The Pieta is just inside and to the right of the entry doors. The centerpiece of St. Peter's is the huge golden altar. Here only the pope can say Mass. Beneath the altar is the gilded tomb of St. Peter himself, the patron saint of Rome. Visitors can go downstairs, where popes and holy men are buried, but the best trip is up to the base of the great dome, where the view of the sanctuary below is dizzying. For the intrepid climber, stairs circle up inside the dome to the very top; for those who wish a less strenuous experience, the roof of the church offers spectacular views.
Piazza San Pietro, open daily.

2. San Giovanni in Laterano.

One of the four Patriarchal Basilicas in Rome, St. John of Lateran is the city's main cathedral. It is the home church of the pope, who is also the Bishop of Rome. St. John's grand façade is balanced by Borromini's classic interior. Standing on the site of Rome's first Christian basilica, the oldest Egyptian obelisk in the city graces St. John's and its adjoining cloisters.

3. Santa Maria Maggiore.

In 352 AD, Pope Liberius had a vision of the Virgin Mary, in which she told him to build a church on the spot where he found snow in summer. As predicted, icy flakes fell on the morning of August 5, and the pope built this great basilica, which features spectacular mosaics and twin domes.
Piazza di Santa Maria Maggiore, open daily.

4. Pantheon.

For almost two thousand years, visitors have marveled that this feat of engineering has remained standing. During the Imperial period,, the Pantheon was a "temple to all the gods;" in the middle ages it became a church. The awe-inspiring interior is lit by a single skylight 140 feet above the floor.
Piazza della Rotonda, open daily.

5. Santa Maria del Popolo.

One of three churches in the Piazza del Popolo, this early Renaissance church houses more great art than some museums: two spectacular Caravaggio masterpieces and the Chigi Chapel, designed by Raphael. Art lovers must be certain not to miss it.

Piazza del Popolo, open daily.

6. Santa Maria in Trastevere.

A medieval masterpiece remarkable for its mosaics, this church is located in the "Greenwich Village of Rome." Expect to see students strumming guitars, fruit sellers, and busy sidewalk cafes in the piazza outside.

Piazza Santa Maria in Trastevere, open daily.

7. Santa Prassede

Near the Santa Maria Maggiore, this church was founded in the 9th century and was decorated with the most important Byzantine mosaics in Rome, reminiscent of the extraordinary mosaics in Ravenna.

Via Santa Prassede 9A, open daily.

8. Santa Croce in Gerusalemme.

Founded in 320AD, the church holds irreplaceable relics from early Jerusalem, including pieces of Christ's Cross (Croce means cross in Italian) and part of Pontius Pilate's inscription in Latin.

Piazza di Santa Croce in Gerusalemme 12, open daily.

9. San Paolo Fuori le Mura.

The fourth of the Patriarchal Basilicas, St Paul's Outside the Walls was completed around 1214, but suffered a terrible fire in 1823. The mosaics in the church, which celebrates Rome's other patron saint, include both 13th century works and a 19th century masterpiece on the façade.

Via Ostiense 186. Open daily.

10. Sant'Andrea al Quirinale.

Known as the "Pearl of the Baroque" because of its roseate marble interior, this church was designed by Bernini and built between 1658-70.

Via del Quirinale 29, open Wed-Mon, closed August.

The Top 10 Things To See At The Vatican

Vatican City has been a sovereign state since the Treaty of Lateran was signed in 1929. The Vatican has its own postal system and its own currency, Vatican lire, which is legal all over Italy. Thanks to massive constructon efforts for Jubilee 2000, visitors will find parking, transportation and sanitary facilities in and around the Vatican much improved. Women should cover shoulders; no shorts for men or women.

1.   The Piazza and Colonnade.

It is thanks to Mussolini that Bernini's spectacular piazza, with its graceful curving colonnade, sets off the massive basilica and soaring dome the way that they do. In the late 1920s, the dictator ordered the demolition of hundreds of crumbling old houses and built the broad avenue of the Via della Conciliazione leading from the river to St. Peter's. It is from a window overlooking this piazza that the pope makes his weekly personal appearance. During the Christmas season this beautiful piazza is decorated with a giant tree and lifesized Nativity scene. At midnight on December 24 the Christmas bells begin to ring and the Pope says a mass, which is broadcast to the crowds in the piazza over giant television screens. To appreciate the symmetry of the piazza, climb to the top of St. Peter's dome for a spectacular view.

2.   The Basilica of St. Peter.

St. Peter's attracts millions of visitors of all different faiths from all over the world. You should be one of them. Keep the crowds in mind, especially during the summer and on major religious holidays. Viewing Michelangelo's dome and his soul satisfying sculpture, The Pieta, are both essential to the experience of visiting St. Peter's. The Pieta is just inside and to the right of the entry doors. You may have to wait patiently for a glimpse, but that wait is well worth it. The centerpiece of St. Peter's is the huge golden altar; here, only the pope can say mass. Beneath the altar is the gilded tomb of St. Peter himself, the patron saint of Rome. Visitors are invited to go downstairs, where popes and holy men are buried, but the best trip is up to the base of the great dome, where the view of the sanctuary below is dizzying. For the intrepid climber, stairs circle up inside the dome to the very top; for those who wish a less strenuous experience, the roof of the church offers a spectacular views of the city.

3. Michelangelo's Pieta.

Art historians say that it was with this incredible sculpture
that Michelangelo's career really began. It was finished in
1499, when he was only 25 years old. Of perfectly white
Carrara marble, the *Pieta* is filled with such tenderness and
emotion that it is hard to believe it was carved from stone.
Attacked by a madman in 1970, the statue is now encased in
bulletproof glass.

4. The Raphael Rooms in the Vatican Museum

Pope Julius chose Raphael to decorate the four rooms of his
papal apartments. The artist and his pupils began the work in
1508, which took over 16 years to complete. The frescoes
established Raphael's reputation in Rome, making him an
equal to Michelangelo, who at the same time was painting the
ceiling of the Sistine Chapel. The works are impossibly
complex and overwhelmingly beautiful.

St. Peter's

5. The Sistine Chapel

The main chapel within the Vatican Museums, its incredible frescoes were executed by Michelangelo, Perugino and Botticelli. Michelangelo's painted ceiling is arguably the greatest artwork on earth, especially now that its colors have been restored to their original vibrance. The fastest route to the Sistine Chapel is a 1.5- hour walk from the main museum entrance through a labyrinth of spectacular collections. Other routes to the Chapel, which encompass the entire museum network within the Vatican, can take all day.

6. The Top of the Dome

Gazing up from inside, the dome of St. Peter's seems to rize forever. Looking down into the rotunda is a dizzying experience. Ascending to the roof, you have the choice of stepping out onto the flat surface that overlooks the great piazza or climbing the narrow, one-way staircase that leads up to the cupola.

7. The Tomb of St. Peter

A simple crypt under the magnificent papal altar holds the remains of St. Peter himself.

8. The Vatican Gardens

A visit to the forty acres of Vatican Gardens must be arranged several days in advance, but it is worth the effort. The tour involves both a bus ride and walking.
Tel. 06 69884466 or fax 06 69885100 to arrange for tickets, which must be picked up at least 24 hours in advance.

9. The Statue of St. Peter

This statue is venerated by the faithful. Once attributed to di Cambio, it is now believed to be a much earlier work. The right foot of the bronze statue has been worn smooth by the hands of pilgrims who have been coming for centuries from all parts of the world. On important feast days the statue is dressed in sumptuous robes and a papal mitre. It is located at the end of the nave.

10. The Vatican Museums

The Vatican Museums' vast network of 1,400 rooms is indicative of the extraordinary artistic riches in the possession of the Catholic church. From the main entrance on the Viale Vaticano, visitors may select from among several itineraries that include: Egyptian, Etruscan, tapestry, map, and sculpture galleries, as well as touring the massive collections of paintings and religious artifacts.

The Top 10 Historic Places to Visit to Step Back in Time

In Rome, history blends with modern day life on almost every corner, where ancient ruins lie next to contemporary buildings. The following is a list of sites that will encourage your imagination to re-visit events that changed the world.

1. Area Sacra

The remains of four temples were discovered here, the oldest of which dates back to the 4th century BC. Behind the temples are the ruins of the Curia of Pompey, where the Senate met and where Julius Caesar was assassinated on 15 March 44 BC. The Area Sacra is home to so many feral cats that a sanctuary has been established at Torre Argentina. Stand on the sidewalk overlooking the Area Sacra and let your mind travel back in history. . . .
Largo di Torre Argentina.

2. The Colosseum

Probably the most impressive monument in the city, it was the site of gladiatorial combats and animal hunts until the 6th century. 50,000 spectators were shielded from the hot Roman sun by a huge awning, called a velarium. Pick a quiet spot and imagine the roar of the crowds, the smell of blood... thumbs up or thumbs down?

3. The Roman Forum

The Forum was the center of life in ancient Rome. Wandering through its vast ruins, you can imagine the noise of the lively market, the hushed political conversation, and the prayerful worshipers in the temples. For your first view, climb the stairs to the Campidoglio at sunset and walk behind city hall to the point that overlooks the Forum. As the setting sun turns the golden marble to pink, and the shadows deepen the green brush, you will see this spectacular ruin in all its glory.

4. The Ardeatine Caves

The site commemorating the Nazi execution of several hundred Romans in 1944. This contemporary memorial is a reminder of the atrocities committed in the course of the twentieth century and is essential to understanding modern Italy.
Via Ardeatina 174

5. The Circus Maximus

Once ancient Rome's largest stadium; today only a grassy esplanade. It remains as a reminder of the horse and chariot races, athletic contests, and wild animal fights staged here. Walk the old racecourse; perhaps you will hear the pounding of hooves, the roar of chariot wheels.

Via del Circo Massimo

6. Santa Maria in Aracoeli and the Aracoeli Staircase

Located on the Capitoline Hill, the church is famous for the Santo Bambino, an olive-wood sculpture of Jesus, which is thought to have miraculous. powers.

7. The Ghetto

Dates back to 1556, when all the Jews of Rome were forced to live inside a high-walled enclosure erected on the order of Pope Paul IV. The inhabitants of the ghetto were allowed out only during the day. Today, the ghetto is a setting for beautiful restaurants and shops, winding streets, and the grand synagogue.

Near the Lungotevere dei Cenci

8. The Pyramid of Caius Cestius

Erected in 12 BC, the pyramid probably looked as incongruous then as it does now. 89 feet high it took almost a year to build. It is set in the Aurealian Wall, dating from the 3rd century AD, near Porta San Paolo. Along with the obelisks that dot the city, the pyramid is a reminder of the Romans' ancient love/hate relationship with Egypt.

9. The Campo de' Fiori

The most vibrant of Roman squares, it has been a meeting place for Romans since the 14th century. In the center of the piazza is a statue of Giordano Bruno, a great philosopher burned in the square during the Inquisition. The market located here is not just for tourists; Romans have been buying their food and flowers here for over 600 years.

10. The Mussolini Effect

Can be seen throughout the city and reminds visitors that the Fascist dictator made a lasting mark. From the Foro Italico, where an obelisk spells out his name, to the broad Via della Conciliazione, which Mussolini built to open up the entrance to St. Peter's basilica, there are reminders of the Fascist regime. The huge EUR building complex west of the city, with its distinctive Fascist-style architecture, houses the Museo della Civilta' Romana, where a detailed and magnificent scale model of ancient Rome is located.

Piazza G. Agnelli 10

The Top 10 Fountains of Rome

In Rome there are even more fountains than churches. Water gurgles, gushes, and sprays, in thousands. Most of them serve as the centerpieces of the innumerable piazzas spread throughout the city. "Meet me at the fountain" is heard a million times a day.

1. Trevi Fountain.

In the 1950s, movies like "Three Coins in a Fountain" epitomized the romance of Rome for a generation of young people. Of course, the title referred to the Trevi, completed in 1762, and the star of other classic films, such as "Roman Holiday" and "La Dolce Vita." Legend says that if you throw a coin into this fountain, you will be assured a return to the Enternal City.
Piazza Fontana di Trevi

2. Fontana dei Fiumi.

Bernini's spectacular fountain in the center of the Piazza Navona features the world's four great rivers as they were known in the mid-1600s: the Ganges, the Danube, the Nile and the River Plate. A powerful piece of sculpture, marking one of Rome's most beautiful piazzas, the Fontana dei Fiumi is a wonderful place to spend the afternoon.
Piazza Navona

3. Piazza San Pietro.

There is a pair of marvelous fountains in this huge piazza. The first was designed by Maderno in 1614. Its twin was built later. A great place to rest after a tour of the basilica.

4. Fontana della Barcaccia.

Located at the foot of the Spanish Steps, this Baroque fountain is often hidden by the hordes of tourists who crowd the piazza. The "leaking boat" is the charming symbol of one of Rome's stylish shopping areas. Don't be surprised if you see a bride in full wedding regalia being photographed in front of the fountain while tourists, taxis, and horse drawn carriages bustle in the background.
Piazza di Spagna

5. Fontana della Tartarughe

Built by several sculptors between 1581 and a century later, this graceful fountain in Trastevere depicts handsome youths helping tortoises into a basin. If you like fountains, it's worth a visit when you're in the neighborhood.
Piazza Mattei

6. Piazza della Bocca della Verita Fountain

An 18th century fountain, its water spills over a craggy rock formation where two tritons hold up a gigantic shell. Across the street is one of Rome's more fun attractions, the Bocca della Verita.
Piazza della Bocca della Verita

7. Fontana delle Naiadi

When this fountain was installed in the Piazza della Repubblica in 1901, its four nude bronze nymphs caused a scandal. Today you would yawn at the idea if you weren't dodging the taxis and buses circling the piazza.
Piazza della Repubblica

8. Piazza del Popolo

Piazza del Popolo is at the confluence of the trio of streets that make up Rome's most elegant shopping area. In the center are marble lions and fountains surrounding an imposing central obelisk. This is one of the best rendevous points in Rome, so you've got to know where it is.
Piazza del Popolo

9. Fontana del Tritone

A Bernini masterpiece that sits in the busy Piazza Barberini near Via Veneto, while its little sister, the Fontana delle Api, also by Bernini, sits quietly in a corner of the square. Make the effort.
Piazza Barberini

10. Fountain of the Four Tiaras

Hidden behind the grand colonnade of St. Peter's, this charming fountain was designed by Lombardi and erected in the early 20th century. It's on the side with the Vatican post office.
Piazza San Pietro

The Top 10 Gardens In And Around Rome

One of the wonderful things about Rome is that it's always green, even in the winter. Along with the burnished pastels of the ancient buildings, the umbrella-shaped Mediterranean pines guarantee a calm and cool respite to the traveler, even on the hottest summer days. No trip to Rome would be complete without a visit to one of the city's spectacular gardens.

1. **Villa Borghese Gardens.**
   The Villa Borghese is actually a pleasure garden laid out in the early 17th century. Rome's version of Central Park, with more old-world romance, and a great place to walk and jog.
   Viale Delle Belle Arte

2. **Janiculum Hill (Gianicolo).**
   The Janiculum is famous for its spectacular views of the city, as well as its lunchtime puppet shows.
   Viale Aldo Fabrizi

3. **The Botanical Gardens**
   Behind the Palazzo Corsini, the Botanical Gardens (Orto Botanico) are known for their impressive collection of orchids, ferns and cactuses.
   Via Corsini, Janiculum Hill

4. **The Vatican Gardens**
   The Vatican Gardens extend for forty acres behind St. Peter's. Tours can be booked with the Vatican Information Office, south side of Piazza San Pietro, 06-69884466.
   Vatican City

5. **Aventine Hill**
   There is a little park on the Aventine Hill, next to the ancient church of Santa Sabina. From the overlook, the view of Rome and St. Peter's is wonderful.
   Via di Santa Sabina

6. **The Villa Doria Pamphilj**
   Rome's largest public park was laid out in the mid-17th century. The park is popular with joggers and dog lovers.
   Via di San Pancrazio

7. **The Pincio Gardens**
   These gardens offer one of the best views of Rome from the terrace overlooking the Piazza del Popolo. The gardens are separated from the gardens of the Villa Borghese by ancient walls.
   Above Piazza del Popolo, Pincio Hill

8. The Parco del Celio

On the Celian Hill, this park contains the beautiful 16th century Villa Celimontana in its center.
Viale del Parco del Celio

9. The Farnese Gardens

On the Palatine Hill, these gardens date back to the 16th century and held one of the first botanical gardens in Europe.
Via di San Gregorio

10. The Colle Oppio park

Though small, it offers wonderful views of the Colosseum and contains the ruins of Nero's Golden House and the Baths of Trajan.
Viale Domus Aurea

The Top 10 Bridges Over The Tiber River

Rome is a city bisected by a river. Its bridges are some of the most beautiful in the world and each has a history of its own. When traveling around the city, it is important to know which bridge to take to reach your destination, since some are only for pedestrians and others are one way.

1. **Ponte Fabricio**

   The oldest original bridge in Rome still in use, the Ponte Fabricio(62 BC) is a pedestrian bridge leading from the Ghetto to the Isola Tiberina, the island in the Tiber. The other bridge to the island, the Ponte Cestio, is inscribed with the names of the Byzantine emperors who restored it in AD 370.

2. **Ponte Rotto**

   Near the Piazza della Bocca della Verita, this ruined and abandoned structure means "broken bridge" in Italian. It was built in the 2nd century BC and named Pons Aemilius.

3. **Ponte Sant'Angelo**

   Medieval pilgrims to St. Peter's crossed the Tiber on this bridge, which is known for the Bernini angels that decorate it. *Pedestrians only.*

4. **Ponte Sisto**

   This bridge was commissioned by Pope Sixtus IV in 1474 to replace an ancient Roman bridge that linked Trastevere to the other side of the city. He paid for it by taxing prostitutes.

5. **Ponte Milvio**

   Called Ponte Mollo (wet bridge) by early Romans, it was the battle of Milvian Bridge in 312 AD that resulted in the imposition of Christianity on Rome. The emperor Constantine's vision of the True Cross during the battle inspired him to share his beliefs with the populace.

6. **Ponte Umberto I**

   From this bridge, which crosses the Tiber upstream of the Castel Sant'Angelo, you can take a really beautiful photo-graph of the castel, the river and the dome of St. Peter's rising in the background.

7. **Ponte Vittorio Emanuele II**

   This bridge connects the Vatican with the rest of the city; one way traffic.

8. Ponte Pr. Amedeo Savoia Aosta

One way traffic to the Vatican from the other side of the city.

9. Ponte Flaminio

A project of Mussolini's government, this monumental white marble bridge is the first upstream bridge on the River Tiber.

10. Ponte Regina Margherita

This bridge connects the shopping district of Cola di Rienzo with the Piazza del Popolo.

The Top 10 Sites Of The Roman Republic And Imperial Rome

Legend has it that the city of Rome was founded by **Romulus** in 753 BC after he bested his brother, Remus. By the second century, Rome controlled the western Mediterranean and by the late third century, she was the most magnificent city in the world.

1. **Temples of the Forum Boarium**
   Located in the Piazza della Bocca della Verita, these ancient Republican temples are rare examples of elements of both Roman and Greek architecture.

2. **Area Sacra at Largo di Torre Argentina**
   This mini-Forum is filled with Roman cats and possibly the ghost of Julius Caesar, who was murdered here 15 March 44 BC.

3. **The Ponte Fabricio**
   The pedestrian bridge to the Tiber Island, it dates from the 1st century.

4. **The Roman Forum**
   The center of life in early Rome, the Roman Forum is the best place to get an overview of early Roman history.

5. **The Palatine**
   The Palatine was home to the great houses of the early Roman emperors, set amid ancient gardens.

6. **The Trajan Markets**
   Rome's first shopping center, it was one of the wonders of the classic world and is one of Rome's best preserved ancient sites, *Via IV Novembre*.

7. **The Pantheon**
   Originally built by Agrippa as his own tomb, the Pantheon, with its magnificently designed dome, was the inspiration for the grand domes of the duomo in Florence and St. Peter's in Rome.

8. **The Colosseum**
   Rome's best-known landmark, the Colosseum sat 50,000 cheering fans who came to watch the gladiators battle each other, as well as wild animals. It is an amazing experience to be there.

9. The Arch of Titus

This magnificent Arch towers over the ruins of the Roman Forum. It was erected in 81 AD to commemorate the Sack of Jerusalem by Emperor Titus.

10. Baths of Diocletian

Built in 298 AD, these baths could hold up to 3,000 people, who met to gossip and relax in the bars, libraries, brothels and sports facilities.

Pont Sant'Angelo

The Top 10 Early Christian Sites In Rome

Early Christian sites permeate the city of Rome, which was a center of Christianity from before the fourth century.

1. The Catacombs

Lining the Appia Antica, vast burial grounds offer fascinating glimpses of life in early Christian Rome.
Appia Antica

2. The Vatican Museums

The Pio-Christian Museum within the Vatican Museums has the best collection of early Christian art.

3. Santa Sabina Church

The 5th century door panel is one of the earliest representations of the crucifiction.
Aventine Hill

4. Santa Costanza Church

The 4th C. mosaic helped to spread the message of early Christianity.
Via Nomentana 349

5. The Pantheon

Now consecrated as a Christian church, the Pantheon was once a temple for all the gods.
Piazza della Rotonda

6. Sant' Agnese Fuori le Mura, 630 AD

Site of a 4th century basilica with a mosaic of the saint.
Via Nomentana 349

7. San Lorenzo fuori le Mura

Erected on the site of Saint Lorenzo's martyrdom, the church has been added to over the centuries.
Piazzale del Verano 3

8. Santo Stefano Rotondo, 5th C.

One of Rome's earliest churches.
Via di Santo Stefano 7

9. Necropoli precostantiniana (scavi), c 320 AD

The excavations under St. Peter's basilica offer a view of early Christian Rome. Apply at the Uffici Scavi, at the Vatican, for permission to enter.

10. Santa Maria Maggiore

Built in 440 AD, this is one of the most complete examples of an early Christian basilica.

The Top 10 Medieval Sites In Rome

A center of power in the eighth and ninth centuries, Rome was afflicted by strife during the tenth, eleventh and twelfth centuries. Violent conflict had left the city poor and desolate. In 1309 the pope moved his headquarters to Avignon. Still, dedicated artists managed to create beauty. The following are the most important medieval sites. Note the references to the Cosmati family, who developed a particular Roman style of decoration worked in marble and decorated with colorful bands of mosaic.

1. **Santa Maria in Trastevere**
   The mosaic façade is the medieval remnant of a church added to over the ages.

2. **Santa Sabina on the Aventine Hill**
   The square bell tower is an example of fine medieval architecture.

3. **Church of San Clemente**
   The fine mosaic and Cosmati floor are important to see.

4. **Santa Maria sopra Minerva**
   Rome's only Gothic church.

5. **Santa Cecilia in Trastevere**
   The Cavallini fresco here is representative of medieval work.

6. **Santa Maria in Cosmedin**
   Cosmati work, including the bishop's throne.

7. **Vatican Museum**
   Including Stefaneschi Triptych (1315), originally painted by Giotto and his pupils as an altarpiece for St. Peter's.

8. **Chapel of St. Zeno**
   Some of the best examples of Byzantine mosaics in Rome *Church of San Prassede.*

9. **San Giovanni in Laterano**
   The Cloister contains a masterpiece of 13th century mosaic work.

10. **St. Peter's Church**
    Charlemagne was crowned emperor of the new Holy Roman Empire here in 800.

The Top 10 Renaissance Sites In Rome

Artists, architects and craftsmen, such as Michelangelo, Bramante, Raphael, and Cellini resided in Rome during the Renaissance. When the headquarters of the pope returned to the city, Rome was transformed by the world's best artists.

1. The Tempietto
Bramante completed this first Renaissance building in Rome on the site where St. Peter is believed to have been crucified.
San Pietro in Montorio

2. Palazzi in the Campo de Fiori area
The streets around the Campo deFiori are filled with Renaissance palazzi, including the Villa Farnese by Michelangelo.

3. Via Giulia
This beautiful street is lined with grand Renaissance palaces.

4. Santa Maria del Popolo church
A typical Renassiance church, it houses two Caravaggio paintings and a chapel by Raphael.

5. The Sistine Chapel
The summit of Renaissance art.

6. The Raphael Rooms at the Vatican Museum
Raphael was Michelangelo's great rival and these frescoed rooms demonstrate why.

7. The *Pieta* by Michelangelo
Commissioned for St. Peter's; one of Michelangelo's first works, it helped to establish his reputation as a genius.

8. Palazzo dei Convertendi
Parts of the earlier Palazzo Caprini by Bramante survive here, near the Vatican.
Via della Conciliazione 43

9. Palazzo del Cancelleria
This is a splendid example of Renaissance architecture.
Piazza della Cancelleria

10. Villa Farnesina
This palace was built for banker Agostino Chigi and is one of the earliest true Renaissance villas.
Via della Lungara 230

The Top 10 Baroque Sites In Rome

Rome was the birthplace of the Baroque movement and the city is filled with prime examples of Baroque art and architecture. The Catholic Church, very wealthy during the 16th century, commissioned luxurious works of art and ornate architecture.

1. Borghese Museum

The Bernini sculptures are simply extraordinary; statues in marble that seem alive.

2. Bernini's Fontana dei Fiumi

The centerpiece of Piazza Navona, this magnificent fountain is one of the most memorable in Rome.

3. Spanish Steps

Designed in 1735, the steps are a splendid public space today.

4. St. Peter's Church

Baldacchino altar and the Monument to Pope Alexander VII, both by Bernini.

5. Pozzo Corridor

Rooms of St. Ignatius near the Gesu church at Piazza del Gesu 45; the use of perspective was a favorite Baroque device, shown to advantage here in these Pozzo frescoes.

6. San Carlo alle Quattro Fontane

This tiny church by Borromini, also known as San Carlino, is one of the great architect's last works.
Quiranal Hill

7. The Gesu Church/ the Church of St. Ignazio

The first Jesuit church to be built in Rome, the design of the Gesu is the epitomy of Baroque. Of particular importance is the chapel designed by the great Jesuit artist, Andrea Pozzo. Two blocks away, Piazza San Ignazio contains Pozzo's fantastic tromp l'oeil cupola.

8. Caravaggio paintings around the city

Rome is the fortunate custodian of a grand collection of Caravaggio paintings. From the Borghese Museum to the Santa Maria del Popolo church, from Sant'Agostino church to the Palazzo Doria Pamphili galleries, Caravaggio paintings are incredible.
San Luigi dei Francesi church, Via Santa Giovanna d'Arco

9. Sant-Agnese in Agone by Borromini

Although the name of this church appears to indicate St. Agnes in agony, it actually refers to the games played in the Piazza Navona in Roman times. Borromini's facade graces the church.

10. Colonnade at St. Peter's Square

This vast piazza was designed by Bernini. It was begun in 1656 and finished in 1667. It isn't a square, but rather an ellipse, framed by huge colonnades, each with four rows of columns.

The Top 10 Places For Children

These places and activities are recommended for families traveling together. Since Romans are particularly partial to children, you will always feel welcome.

1. **"Conoscriroma, A guide to Roma for curious children"**
   A brochure of itineraries especially planned for children, available free at green tourist information kiosks.

2. **The Janiculum Hill**
   Rome's largest terrace with a merry-go-round and puppet theatre. Everyday at noon a cannon is shot off beneath the terrace at Piazzale Garibaldi.

3. **Villa Pamphili**
   Over 500 acres of grassy meadows, perfect for kite flying, bike paths, and a roller-skating rink.
   Via San Pancrazio

4. **Villa Torlonia**
   Looks like the witch's house in Hansel and Gretel. Extraordinary glass windows imbedded with the images of owls, swallows and bats.
   Via Nomentana 70

5. **Bocca della Verita, The "Mouth of Truth"**
   Church of Santa Maria in Cosmedin, Piazza della Bocca della Verita. According to ancient legend, it bites the hand of anyone who tells a lie.

6. **Villa Borghese**
   Downtown park, children's cinema, bike rentals, pony rides, rowboats for rent in the Giardino del Lago.

7. **Giardino Zoologico,**
   The Zoo of Rome.
   Viale del Giardino Zoologico

8. **Catacombs of San Sebastian**
   Closed Thursdays, fascinating underground cemetery with mysterious passages and tunnels.
   Via Appia Antica

9. **Roman Forum**
   Where the ancient Romans met and talked.

10. **Roman Colosseum**
    Where the gladiators fought.

Rome's Seven Hills Plus Three

Rome is a city built around seven hills. By the 8th century BC, shepherds and farmers still lived on four of the seven. Over the last three millennia, Rome has grown to encompass all seven major hills, and an additional three minor ones, as well as the flat lands far beyond. Here is a list of all ten hills.

1. Aventine

The Aventine area is one of the most elegant residential areas in Rome today, offering spectacular views across the city. High on the Aventine are the Basilica of Santa Sabina (AD 422), the Church of Santi Bonifacio e Allessio, and the Piazza dei Cavalieri di Malta, famous for the bronze keyhole through which one can see a miniature view of the dome of St. Peter's far below.

2. Capitoline

The Capitoline Hill, overlooking the Forum, was named the "caput mundi" to symbolize the city's place at the head of the world. Today, the Capitoline is the site of the 12th century City Hall, as well as the outstanding Capitoline Museums. The piazza, designed by Michelangelo, boasts a magnificent statue of Marcus Aurelius at the center.

3. The Celian Hill

Overlooks the Colosseum and, in Imperial Rome, was the fashionable place to live. Today, it is a parklike Archaeological Zone filled with old churches and temples, including the Santo Stefano Rotondo, the oldest circular church in Italy.

4. The Esquiline

The largest and highest of Rome's seven hills, it has been one of the poorest quarters of the city since the days of the Empire. It is, however, home to the magnificent basilica of Santa Maria Maggiore, as well as celebrated smaller churches: Santa Prassede, San Pietro in Vincoli, and Santa Prudenziana. Nearby are the remains of the Baths of Trajan.

5. The Palatine Hill

Was a very desirable place to live in ancient Rome - its inhabitants included Cicero, Catullus, the emperor Augustus and his successors, Tiberius, Caligula and Domitian. According to legend, Romulus and Remus were raised in a cave on the Palatine by a she-wolf. The area is green and park-like, full of excavations revealing early Rome.

6. The Quiranale

Was a residential area in Imperial times. Today the grand Palazzo del Quiranale is home to the president of Italy. Although the palace is not open to the public, the giant Roman statues of Castor and Pollux in the piazza are worth seeing, as well as the views of the city below.

7. The Viminale

There is nothing much on this hill except for houses. Its fame lies only in the fact that Italian school children must memorize the seven hills of Rome.

8. The Janiculum

Overlooking the Tiber, on the Trastevere side of the river, it played a major role in the city's defense. The huge park at the top of the hill is filled with monuments to Garibaldi, as well as puppet theatres, gelaterie, and other amusements for families and children.

9. The Pincio Hill

Above the Piazza del Popolo, the Pincio Gardens were designed by Valadier in the early 19th century atop earlier gardens planted by ancient Romans. From the Piazza Napoleone I, there is a panoramic view of the city, especially romantic and beautiful at sunset. Within the park is a 19th century water clock, a fascinating design by a Dominican monk and one of two in the city.

10. Monte Mario

The hill that runs across the city to the north. From the Café Zodiaco or the Cavalieri Hilton atop Monte Mario, the view of the city is spectacular. From below, one can see the observatory and the gigantic statue of Christ that blesses the city. On the Via Camellucia, which runs along the hill, there are diplomatic residences, convents, and beautiful walled villas.

The Top 10 Most Beautiful Piazzas of Rome

Many European cities are built around squares, but the Roman piazzas are the most beautiful of all. Each one was an opportunity for the artists and architects of the time to show off their work in the midst of public spaces. There's nothing more satisfying than sipping coffee in a sidewalk café, watching the people, the fountains, and obelisks of a busy Roman piazza.

1. Piazza Navona

This is the most wonderful piazza in Rome, the site of Bernini's great fountain, Michelangelo's architecture, the Christmas festival, the soaring obelisk, and dozens of restaurants and bars. People throng here day and night, winter and summer. If you don't come, you haven't been to Rome.

2. Campo de' Fiori

For over a thousand years, people have come to this piazza to buy their flowers, fish, and vegetables. The statue of the martyred Father Bruno watches the bustle of Roman life continue in the 21st century.

3. Piazza del Popolo

A grand piazza with room for strolling, resting, or sipping coffee it is also the beginning of the trio of shopping streets – Via Ripetta, Via Corso, and Via Babuino, that lead to the Spanish Steps.

4. Piazza di Spagna

Called the Piazza di Spagna because it is the location of the Spanish embassy to the Vatican. The Spanish Steps lead up to the Trinita dei Monti church above. In the spring, azaleas line the steps, which are filled all year long with lounging students, exhausted tourists, and more than a few poets and musicians.

5. Area Sacra, Largo di Torre Argentina

This mini-forum holds the remains of four temples, all dating to the era of the Roman Republic. What makes it special to the visitor is that this is the actual site of the murder of Julius Caesar. It is also home to dozens of Rome's feral cats.

6. Piazza Venezia

Piazza Venezia isn't one of those places you would go for a quiet cup of coffee; you might get run over by a bus. The buildings that surround the piazza make it interesting enough to take the risk. First is Il Vittoriano, the gigantic, white marble monument finished in 1911 to honor the first king of the unified Italy. Derisively called "The Wedding Cake," or the "Typewriter," it looms over the piazza as a reminder of self-important architecture. The Palazzo Venezia, across the Piazza, houses a first class collection of Renaissance paintings. Mussolini used the building as his headquarters and spoke to the public from a balcony on the second floor.

7. Piazza della Rotonda

Centered by the Pantheon, this piazza is a favorite of visitors to Rome, who sit at the sidewalk cafes (or at McDonald's), people-watching and enjoying the ancient settings. Here, you will see souvenir kiosks and newsstands, nuns and students, traffic police and, once a year, the runners of the Rome Marathon, who pant their way past the columns of the Pantheon.

8. Campidoglio

Said to be the most perfectly designed public space in the world, Michelangelo's piazza is surrounded by the Capitol building, as well as the Capitoline Museums. Centering the intricate design of paving stones is the magnificent bronze statue of Marcus Aurelius. Since there is a civic wedding chapel on this piazza, often you will see brides and grooms awaiting their turn to go inside to be married.

9. Piazza Colonna

The reason to go to this piazza is the 100-foot-high Column of Marcus Aurelius, erected in AD 180. The intricate carvings chronicle the German War (AD171-3), and the Sarmatic War (AD 174-5). It is amazing to see the emperor's campaigns documented in the spiraling carvings decorating the 12-foot in diameter marble column.

10. Piazza Santa Maria in Trastevere

This piazza is the heart of the ancient quarter of Trastevere-- the octagonal fountain and Santa Maria in Trastevere church are augmented by sidewalk cafes and ice cream vendors, which are crowded, day and night, all year. Trastevere is the Greenwhich Village of Rome, and this piazza is its Washingtgon Square.

The Top 10 Places in Rome Connected to Michelangelo

1. The Piazza del Campidoglio.
Designed by Michelangelo at the behest of Pope Paul III, this piazza is said to be the most perfect public space ever built.

2. St. Peter's
The largest, most magnificent church in Christendom, St. Peter's soars above the Vatican Hill, crowned by Michelangelo's huge dome.
Piazza San Pietro

3. Palazzo Farnese
The most imposing Italian palace of the 16th century, this is another of Michelangelo's masterpieces. Currently the site of the French Embassy in Rome, the palazzo is open to visitors one day a week, by advance appointment. It is worth seeing for the Carracci frescoes, which are said to rival the ceiling of the Sistine Chapel.
Piazza Farnese

4. The Sistine Chapel
The main chapel inside the Vatican Museums, its incredible frescoes were painted by Michelangelo, Perugino and Botticelli. Michelangelo's painted ceiling is arguably the greatest artwork on earth, especially now that its colors have been restored to their original vibrance. The fastest route to the Sistine Chapel is a 1.5 hour walk from the main museum entrance, through a labyrinth of spectacular collections. Other routes to the Chapel, which encompass the entire museum network within the Vatican, can take all day. There is a nice cafeteria inside the complex, an enclosed garden, and refreshment bars. Restrooms are convenient. The Raphael rooms and the map gallery are particularly impressive. Don't let long waiting lines outside keep you away the museum is huge and can accommodate thousands of visitors a day.
Citta' del Vaticano (Vatican City), open daily except for religious and public holidays (there are many); free last Sunday of the month.

5. The *Pieta* at St. Peter's

Art historians say that this incredible sculpture launched Michelangelo's career as an artist par excellence. Of perfect, white, Carrara marble, the Pieta is filled with such tenderness and emotion that it is hard to believe it was carved from stone. Attacked by a madman in 1970, the statue is now encased in bulletproof glass.
Piazza San Pietro.

6. The Moses in St. Pietro in Vincoli Church

An extraordinarily powerful work, Michelangelo's statue of Moses is less famous than the *Pieta*, but worth seeing for its strength and authority. Freud wrote a treatise on this sculpture as part of his work on Moses.
Piazza di San Pietro in Vincoli, 4a

7. The Cappella Sforza (chapel) in the Bascilica of Santa Maria Maggiore

Built by Giacomo Della Porta from a design by Michelangelo, it was the inspiration for other "sculpted" interiors by Bernini and Borromini.
Piazza di Santa Maria Maggiore

8. Portrait of Michelangelo

Housed in the Palazzo Gaddi, where Michelangelo lived at one time, is a portrait by Jacopino del Conte of the artist as an old man. This section of Rome was where the flourishing Tuscan colony lived during the 16th century. Michelangelo would have felt at home here.
Via dei Banco di Santo Spirito, 42

9. The Church of Santa Maria degli Angeli

This church was incorporated into the Baths of Diocletian by Michelangelo in 1563, but was altered in the 18th century by Luigi Vanvitelli. An exhibition in the sacristy illustrates the details of Michelangelo's original design.
Via Cernaia, 9

10. The Risen Christ in Santa Maria Sopra Minerva Church

Among the splendid works of art by Bernini and the tombs of St. Catherine of Siena and Fra Angelico, there is the sculpture of the Risen Christ by Michelangelo, considered by some their least favorite of Michelangelo's works. The nude statue of Christ may be unsettling to some, but it is inspirational to many others as a proclamation of the Resurrection
Piazza della Minerva, 42

The Top 10 Things To Do In Trastevere

Trastevere is the Greenwich Village of Rome. It is filled with narrow winding streets and ancient buildings. Aside from the important churches located there, Trastevere is known for its restaurants, bars, art galleries, sidewalk cafes, and boutiques. It is a wonderful place to spend a day or evening.

1. Have a Drink in the Piazza Santa Maria

Sitting in an outdoor café eating gelato or having a drink is a great way to pick up the ambience that is Trastevere. The church and fountain that centers the piazza are important Roman landmarks.

2. Visit the Church of Santa Maria

This old church is the first known to have been dedicated to the virgin mother. The tower is Romanesque, the mosaics on the façade are 12th century, and the portico was built in 1702. The three doors are Roman entabulatures. The church is truly a reflection of the various ages of Roman history.

3. Go to the Movies In English at Cinema Pasquino

Sometimes you just have to hear some English and this is the place to go. Renovated in the mid-1990s, the Pasquino shows first run movies in English on its two screens everyday.

4. Wander the Tiny, Ancient Streets

Narrow cobbled passageways, the streets of Trastevere are endlessly fascinating. The Via della Lungaretta, in particular, is a good street to explore for a glimpse of ancient Rome and to find more than a few good restaurants.

5. Go to Europe's Largest Flea Market in Porta Portese (Sunday Mornings)

Porta Portese is the mother of all flea markets. Take the bus (expect it to be packed) and wander there, through a kilometer of stalls filled with antiques, clothes, kitchen utensils, pet supplies, furniture, rugs, hardware, lamps, and much more.

6. See the Tomb of Saint Cecilia

St. Cecilia was an aristocrat and is now the patron saint of music. She was martyred in AD 230. Her attackers first tried scalding her to death for practicing Christianity and then beheaded her; she sang through both events. Her body, which was missing for centuries, was found in the Catacombs of San Callisto and is now in the church of Santa Cecilia in Trastevere, in the Piazza di Santa Cecilia.

7. Sample the Dozens of Restaurants

The neighborhood is filled with good restaurants, including La Tana di Noantri (via della Paglia,1/2/3), the Pizzeria Panottoni (viale Trastevere 53), or the Spirito diVino (via dei Genovesi 31A), along with dozens of pizzerias and trattorias.

8. Shop the Varied Boutiques

In Trastevere there are art galleries and bookstores, clothing boutiques and souvenir shops.

9. View the Architecture of Rome's Oldest Neighborhood

Some of Rome's most fascinating churches are in Trastevere: Santa Maria in Trastevere, Santa Cecilia in Trasevere, San Francesco a Ripa, Santa Maria della Scala, and San Crisogono among them. The Casa della Gioventu, the former headquarters of the Fascist Youth organization, was designed by Luigi Moretti and introduces plasticity in concept and form. The Torre degli Anguillara (13th century) is only one of the many medieval towers that dotted Trastevere.

10. Visit the Museum Drugstore and Columbaria

This combination of supermarket, bar, and disco also houses a group of columbaria (walls lined with burial niches) that date back to ancient Rome. This is a new way of preserving archaelogical remains: building around them instead of burying them.

The Top 10 Obelisks Around Rome

Obelisks, a structural design originally from Egypt, date from the early history of Rome. Many were commissioned by Roman emperors and others were brought to the city by triumphant armies.

1. **Obelisk of Santa Maria sopra Minerva**
    Egyptian obelisk held up by Bernini's elephant.

2. **Obelisk of Piazza San Giovanni in Laterano**
    The oldest obelisk in Rome, dating from the 15th century BC.

3. **Obelisk of Piazza del Popolo**
    Dates from the 12-13th C. BC. Earlier erected in the Circus Maximus.

4. **Obelisk of Piazza Montecitorio**
    One of Augustus' war trophies.

5. **Obelisk of Piazza del Esquilino**
    First stood at the entrance to Augustus' tomb.

6. **Obelisk of Piazza del Quirinale**
    First stood at the Mausoleum of Augustus.

7. **Obelisk of Axum**
    Brought from Ethiopia by Mussolini's army.
    Near Circus Maximus

8. **Trajan's Column**
    Inaugurated by Trajan in 113AD. Though technically not an obelisk, it is extraordinary.
    Via dei Fori Imperiali

9. **Fontana dei Fiumi**
    Piazza Navona

10. **Obelisk of Piazza San Pietro**

The Top 10 Historic Places Related To Artist/Writers In Rome

1. **Via del Corso 20**
   Home of J.W. Goethe.

2. **Baths of Caracalla**
   Site where Percy B. Shelley wrote *Prometheus Unbound*.

3. **The American Academy**
   An association whose members have included Michael Graves, John Russell Pope, Samuel Barber, Frank Stella, and many others.
   Via Angelo Masina 5

4. **Cinecitta Film Studios**
   Production site of Italian Neo-Realism films, later a center for international productions.

5. **The Protestant Cemetery**
   Contains the graves of Keats and Shelley.
   Via Caio Cestio 6

6. **The Villa Medici (French Academy)**
   The Prix de Rome prize brought musicians like Berlioz, Bizet and Debussy to Rome to compose here.

7. **Tivoli**
   The little town outside of Rome where Franz Liszt lived and worked.

8. **The Keats and Shelley Memorial House**
   Piazza di Spagna

9. **Lord Byron, Goethe and Victor Hugo statues**
   Villa Borghese Gardens

10. **Casina di Raffaello**
    Raphael's summerhouse.
    Villa Borghese Gardens

The Top 10 Graves To See In Rome

1. John Keats and Percy Bysshe Shelley
Great English poets who came to complete their classical education and to be inspired by the city.
Protestant Cemetery
Via Caio Cestio 6

2. Romulus, the First King of Rome
Near the Comitium in the Roman Forum, the tombstone is inscribed with early Latin characters.
Protestant Cemetery

3. Tomb of St. Peter
Only recently have scholars verified this to be the actual tomb of Peter.
Vatican

4. The Pantheon
Agrippa built this extraordinary, domed temple to be his own grave. Today it houses the bones of the great artist Raphael, as well as the kings of Italy.

5. Capuchin Cemetery with its 4,000 skeletons
The monks here fashioned lamps and furniture out of their dearly departed colleagues, and then relaxed with a cappuccino (named after the color of their robes).
Santa Maria della Concezione
Via Veneto 27

6. Cecilia Metella
This drum shaped tomb was restored for the Jubilee 2000.
Via Appia Antica, III Miglio

7. The Catacombs which line the Via Appia Antica
There are the graveyards of ancient Christians as well as others from ancient Rome. It is a fascinating experience to walk the dim, dank passages, which date back thousands of years. Most catacombs offer guided tours in several languages.

8. Mausoleum of Augustus

This weedy hill between the river and Via Corso was once the most prestigious place in Rome. It was built by Emperor Augustus in 28 BC; today it is the end of numerous bus lines. The emperor's ashes, however, still rest where they have lain since 14 AD. The magnificent friezes and bas reliefs celebrate the victory of Augustus over Gaul and Spain in 13 BC. Next to the tomb is the glass-walled Ara Pacis (altar of peace).
Piazza Augusto Imperatore

9. Hadrian's Tomb (the Castel Sant' Angelo)

Now part of the Vatican complex, the Castel Sant'Angelo was constructed to be the tomb of the emperor Hadrian in 139 AD. Standing on the edge of the river, it is one of the most memorable sites in Rome.
Lungotevere Castello

10. Pyramid of Caius Cestius

Like others of his time, Roman praetor Caius Cestius wanted an impressive tomb. This pyramid sits incongruously in the Aurelian Wall, near Porta San Paolo, as it has since 12 BC.
Porta San Paolo

The Top 10 Reference And Rendevous Points In Central Rome

1. **Lungotevere**
   Road along the river; each section of the road on each side of the river has a name.
   i.e. Lungotevere Acqua Acetosa

2. **Piazza di Spagna**

3. **The Spanish Steps**

4. **Piazza del Popolo**
   A central point for taxis, buses, and trams.

5. **Piazza San Silvestro**
   A central point for buses.

6. **Piazza Repubblica**
   Near the main train station.

7. **Castel Sant' Angelo (Hadrian's Tomb)**
   On the lungotevere near St. Peter's.

8. **Piazza Risorgimento**
   Near St. Peter's

9. **Piazza Navona**

10. **Piazza Augusto Imperatore**
    Near lungotevere and Via Condotti shopping, a central point for buses.

The Top 10 Information Kiosks In Rome

In the 1990s, the city of Rome built a series of identical green information kiosks. They are open daily and serviced by staff who speak English. Printed information in English is available to visitors free of charge.

1. **Castel Sant Angelo**
   Piazza Pia

2. **Fori Imperiali**
   Piazza del Tempio della Pace

3. **Via del Corso**
   Largo Goldoni

4. **Piazza Navona**
   Piazza Cinque Lune

5. **Via Nazionale**
   Palazzo delle Esposizioni

6. **Trastevere**
   Piazza Sonnino

7. **San Giovanni**
   Piazza S. Giovanni in Laterano

8. **Via del Corso**
   Via Minghetti

9. **Piazza della Repubblica**
   Via Parigi 5

10. **Stazione Termini**
    Piazza dei Cinquecento

The Top 10 Music And Theatre Venues In Rome

For information about tickets, call the Rome Call Center, 06 3600 4399. English-speakers are available from 9 a.m. until 7 p.m. Theatre tickets can be purchased over the telephone with a credit card through Citta Facile «Hallo Ticket» line, 800 907080, Monday through Friday, 10 a.m. - 5 p.m. Pop concert tickets are available from Orbis, Piazza Esquilino, 37, 06 4827915; Prontospettacolo, 06387297; or Box Office, Viale Giulio Cesare 88, 063720215.

1. **National Academy of Santa Cecilia**
   The top music conservatory in Rome and a major concert institution. Box office opens Friday mornings at 9:30 a.m.
   Via della Conciliazione, 4, Tel 06 3234775

2. **RAI, Italian Broadcasting Corporation**
   Concert season, various venues.

3. **Rome Philharmonic Academy**
   Concerts at Teatro Olimpico.
   Piazza Gentile da Fabriano, 17, Tel 06 393304.

4. **Teatro dell' Opera**
   December - June; open air season, July - August.
   Via Firenze 62, Tel 06481601

5. **Ford Entertainment**
   Theatre in English, various venues, «Friday Night Live».
   Tel 064441375

6. **Concerti del Tempietto**
   Classical music.
   www.tempietto.com, Tel 064814800

7. **Tor di Valle Music Village**
   Summer music village.
   Via del Mare km.9.300, Tel 065200356

8. **Teatro di Roma**
   Various venues.
   Tel 0668804601

9. **Church Concerts**
   Information available in Wanted in Rome and Trova Roma publications.

10. **Oratorio del Gonfalone**
    Focuses on Baroque music.
    Via del Gonfalone 32A, Tel 066875952

The Top 10 Places To Go For Sports Activities

1. **Circolo Golf di Roma**
   Via Appia Nuova 716a
   Tel 06786129

2. **Bowling Brunswick**
   Lungotevere Acqua Acetosa 10
   Tel 068086147

3. **Olgiata Golf Club**
   Largo Olgiata 15
   Tel 0630889141

4. **Sheraton Golf Parco de' Medici**
   Viale Parco de' Medici 20
   Tel 066553477

5. **Villa Borghese Park**
   Jogging.

6. **Roman Sport Center**
   Gym, Squash.
   Villa Borghese and Largo Somalia
   Tel 063201667

7. **Rome Pony Club**
   Horseback-riding.
   Via dei Campi Sportivi 43
   Tel 068079709 or www.cavallo.web.it

8. **Sheraton Hotel**
   Squash.
   Via del Pattinaggio, Tel 065453

9. **Villa Ada park**
   Bike paths, pony rides, carousel.
   Entrances on Via Salaria, Via Ponte Salario, Largo Bangladesh

10. **Cycling in Italy**
    www.cycling.it

The Top 10 English Language Religious Institutions In Rome

1. **Anglican**
   All Saints' Anglican Church
   Via del Babuino 153/b, Tel. 0636001881

2. **Baptist**
   Rome Baptist Church
   Piazza S. Lorenzo in Lucina 35, Tel. 066876652

3. **Episcopal**
   St. Paul's within the Walls
   Via Nazionale, corner Via Napoli, Tel. 064883339

4. **Methodist**
   Ponte S. Angelo Methodist Church
   Piazza Ponte S. Angelo, Tel. 066868314

5. **Presbyterian**
   St. Andrew's Presbyterian Church
   Via XX Settembre 7, Tel. 064827627

6. **Catholic**
   Santa Susanna Church
   Via XX Settembre 15, Tel. 0642014554

7. **Church of Jesus Christ of Latter Day Saints**
   Piazza Carnaro 20, Tel. 068272708

8. **Jewish**
   Comunita' Ebraica, Tempio Maggiore
   Lungotevere Cenci, Tel. 066840061

9. **Christian Science**
   c/o Notegen (downstairs)
   Via del Babuino 159, Tel. 06301

10. **Interdenominational**
    Jesus Cares Ministries
    Via del Banco di S. Spirito 3, Tel. 066868233

The Top 10 American And British Financial Institutions In Rome

Most banks in Rome are open 8:30 a.m. to 1:30 p.m. and re-open between 3 and 4. Monday through Friday.

1. **American Express Bank**
   Near the Spanish Steps

2. **Thomas Cook**
   Via del Corso, 23

3. **Chemical Bank**
   Via Bertoloni, 26/b

4. **Citibank**
   Via Abruzzi, 2/4

5. **Morgan Guaranty Trust of New York**
   Via Po, 23

6. **Manufacturers Hanover Trust Company New York**
   Viale Liegi, 10

7. **Barclay's Bank International**
   Via Mercadante, 32

8. **Abbey National Bank**
   Via Appia Nuova, 635

9. **Western Union/Money Transfer**
   Piazza IV Novembre, 1

10. **Merrill Lynch**
    Largo della Fontanella Borghese, 19

The Top 10 Eccentric Sites to Visit In Rome

1. Convento dei Cappuccini

Here the Cappuchin monks, in addition to inspiring the invention of cappuccino, saved the bones of their forebears and made them into room décor.
Via Veneto 27

2. The National Museum of Pasta Foods

Charming, interesting and educational, this little museum is well worth a visit.
Piazza Scanderberg 177

3. The Priory of the Knights of Malta

Through the keyhole in the front door, you can see the dome of St. Peter's perfectly framed in the distance.
Piazza dei Cavalieri di Malta

4. The Pyramid of Caius Cestius

This imposing white marble pyramid set into the Aurelian Wall is an incongruous landmark that celebrates a man known for nothing else. But, it's the only pyramid in the city.
Piazzale Ostiense

5. The Bocca della Verita

Stick your hand in the ancient stone mouth and if you are a liar, it will bite it off. Great fun for both adults and children.
Church of Santa Maria in Cosmedin
Piazza della Bocca Verita

6. The underground basilica at the Church of San Clemente

Under this little church is the original basilica, and under that, is the Mithraeum, the temple of the old mystery religion; under that is an ancient sewer. An opportunity to see the over three thousand years of Roman history in a nutshell.
Via San Giovanni in Laterano

7. Pie' di Marmo

This giant marble foot is a remnant of an ancient statue – don't buy the postcard until you've seen the real thing.
Via del Santo Stefano del Cacco

8. Museo Storico Nazionale dell'Arte Sanitaria

This is the site of the museum of medical history in Italy. It's weirdly fascinating.
Lungotevere in Sassia 3
Piazza Mattei

9. Piazza San Pietro

If you stand on one of two spots marked in the center of the piazza in the front of St. Peter's, the columns of the huge colonnade will miraculously line up perfectly.

10. The Fontana delle Tartarughe

Probably the funkiest fountain in Rome, it stars a group of modest little creatures rather than the heroic, historic, or hulking statues in the other fountains.

The Top 10 Trips To Take Outside Rome

The green tourist information kiosks dotted around Rome offer information on day trips outside the city, including transportation information. Most of the list below can be reached by bus.

1. Ostia, Port of the Empire, and Ostia Antica
Wonderfully preserved temples, frescoed houses, baths, barracks and warehouses from the 4th century BC.

2. Villa d'Este and gardens, Tivoli
The most fantastic villa and gardens in Italy.

3. Villa Gregoriana, Tivoli
Shady paths and gardens surrounding a cardinal's dream villa.

4. Hadrian's Villa, Tivoli
The grandest palace complex ever built in Italy.

5. Frascati
The nearest town of the Castelli Romani area, and nearby Grottaferrata - charming towns in the wine area near Rome.

6. Castel Gandolfo
The summer home of the popes, on the Via Appia Antica, and the beautiful Lake Nemi.

7. Ninfa
Called the "medieval Pompei," was abandoned in the 17th century.

8. Bolsena
On the lake formed by an extinct volcano, is furnished with its own fairy-tale castle.

9. Tarquinia
The city of the Etruscans, with its ancient Necropolis and the "Etruscopolis," an underground park with a reconstruction of the ancient city.

10. Parco di Mostri (Park of the Monsters)
In Bomarzo, created 500 years ago by Prince Orsini as his garden.

Top 10 Most Famous Roman Emperors

From 27 BC until Rome's fall in 476 AD, Rome was ruled by emperors.

1. Augustus

Caesar Augustus (Octavian), styled himself 'first citizen' rather than emperor. His reign was the longest of the caesars (27 BC – 14 AD).

2. Claudius

Under Claudius (41-54 AD), Rome invaded Britain.

3. Nero

Fiddled while Rome burned. Ruler from 54-68 AD, Nero built the incredible Golden House on the Palatine Hill.

4. Titus

Emperor from 79-81 AD, Titus conquered Jerusalem in 70 , burning the city and killing thousands. The disaster at Pompei occurred during his reign.

5. Trajan (98-117)

His name is on the market and the column that documents his victories. Conquered Dacia and the region north of the Danube.

6. Hadrian

An artist and poet, Hadrian (117-138), rebuilt the Pantheon and left his mark on the city with his own magnificent tomb.

7. Marcus Aurelius

Rome's philosopher-king, Marcus Aurelius (161-180) spent his last years on the Danubian frontier. The second-century statue in his honor centers the Campodoglio piazza.

8. Caracalla

Caracalla (211-217) granted citizenship to almost all the free, male inhabitants of the empire and built the Baths on 26 acres.

9. Diocletian

Diocletian (284-305) restored the strength of the emperor's office and eventually selected a co-emperor. The two divided the empire into eastern and western sections.

10. Constantine

The first Christian emperor, Constantine (307-337) reunited the empire and selected Constantinople, as the new capital.

The Top 10 Historic Figures Connected To Rome

1. Romulus and Remus
The King of Alba, threw his nephews into the Tiber. Rescued by a she-wolf, who raised them as her own. Romulus was the first king of Rome.

2. Julius Caesar
Assassinated shortly after being named dictator for life.

3. Emperor Augustus
The nephew of Julius Caesar, Augustus became Rome's first emperor in 27 BC.

4. Emperor Nero
Legend says he watched Rome burn in 64 AD.

5. Mussolini
Italy's dictator for over twenty years, beginning in 1922, Mussolini took the country into World War II as allies of Nazi Germany.

6. Mark Antony
Led Rome as part of the Second Triumvirate, 43 – 32 BC. Mark Antony is also known as Cleopatra's lover.

7. Lucrezia Borgia
Daughter of Pope Alexander VI, Lucrezia had the reputation of inviting men to dinner in order to poison them.

8. Paulina Borghese
Sister of Napoleon, Paulina Borghese posed for the most famous work in the Borghese Museum collection, the Venus Vincitrix.

9. Michelangelo
Possibly the greatest artist the world has known. Responsible for the ceiling of the Sistine Chapel, as well as architectural masterpieces throughout the city.

10. St. Peter
The patron saint of Rome, St. Peter was the inspiration for St. Peter's Basilica, the world's greatest church.

The Top 10 Things To Know To Plan Your Trip To Rome

1. **Rome is a walking city,** despite the millions of cars and buses that clog the streets. Pack comfortable shoes.

2. **Unlike Parisians,** Romans are delighted when you try to speak their language. Brush up your Italian before you go.

3. **Italians are sad** when they see tourists who are afraid to try something new. Don't stick to the old standbys, such as spaghetti bolognese. Ask the waiter to bring you the specialty of the house.

4. **Avoid tourist menus.** They rarely offer good food and the portions are often small.

5. **Plan so that your itinerary makes the most of the area you have decided to tour.** Rome is huge and lack of planning means lost time traversing the city. Try to balance museum visits with outdoor touring so you don't burn out the first day.

6. **Think about your wardrobe.** Pack smart casual, rather than t-shirts and torn jeans. Be sure that you have clothing to cover legs and shoulders if you are planning to visit churches. Carry a light shawl or scarf with you in case you change your plans and need a cover up.

7. **If you are traveling with a laptop computer,** keep in mind that the electrical plug is going to be different, as will the voltage. The phone plug will be different as well. Bring along an adapter (if your computer works on both 110 and 220), as well as different plugs sizes (the European Union does not have standard sizes on their dual pin plugs). For the telephone, you can often pick up an adapter plug in a telephone or hardware store. Sometimes, a hotel with newer phones will have a phone wire that fits into your modem.

8. **Phone cards are available** for cellphones, as well as for pay phones. There are international phone cards good for making calls back home. Your own telephone credit card can be accessed by using a local free number. Get the number before you leave home.

9. **Remember that sitting outside** in a café or bar can cost twice the price of standing at the bar inside.

10. **There are internet cafes located in and around Rome;** if you have your own computer, there are free servers at www.iol.it and www.tiscalinet.it that you can download before leaving home if your own server doesn't have European access.

10 Things To Know About Security In Rome

Rome is no more dangerous than any large American city and often less so. Still, it's smart to be aware. Take the hints below to ensure your visit is not marred by avoidable incidents.

1. **Avoid bus number 64 if you can;** it is full of tourists. If you have to take it, be careful of pickpockets.

2. **Watch your things when traveling in a Metro train.** There are those who snatch packages and purses.

3. **Beware of the bands of children** on the Via Corso and near the Colosseum. One will try to distract you, while another will take your wallet or watch.

4. **If someone approaches you late at night** and offers to show you a late night bar, be wary. You may end up with a huge bill that doesn't belong to you.

5. **Lock your car** and hide any valuables.

6. **Leave your valuables** in the hotel safe.

7. **Your hotel will ask for your passport and then return it to you;** keep it in an inside pocket if you need to change money or want to register for a VAT tax return. If you do lose it, it can be reissued in one tense day at the US Consulate. Make sure you have a copy of your passport in a safe place.

8. **Taxis leaving from the official airport departure site are controlled;** ask the price before you get in the car.

9. **Report any thefts to the nearest police or carabinieri station.** The central police station, Via San Vitale 15, has intrepreters who speak English. There are three police forces in Rome: the regular police, the military police (carabinieri) and the traffic police.

10. **Lost credit cards should be reported immediately to:**
    Visa, largo del Tritone, 161, Tel. 0667181
    American Express, Piazza di Spagna, 38, Tel. 068415282
    Diner's Club, piazza Cavour, 25, Tel. 063213841
    Mastercard toll free number, 167 870866.
    Or, call the number on your credit card, collect.

The Top 10 Things To Know About Money In Rome

1. **Now that Italy has joined the EU, and will be using the Euro,** prices are displayed in both Lire and Euros. As of January 1, 2002, the Euro will become the official currency in Italy.

2. **Don't be dismayed if it is as difficult to get into some banks as it is to break into Fort Knox.** Almost every Roman bank has stringent security procedures in place, including revolving glass entry booths and lockers in the lobby, in which you are expected to lock your packages before entering.

3. **Exchange rates are better at banks and ATMs.** If you are changing money, you will need your passport.

4. **Travelers checks can be cashed free of charge** at American Express near Piazza di Spagna, if you don't mind the crowds.

5. **A 15% tip is included in your restaurant bill,** but in Rome it is customary to leave 5-10% more in cash on the table if the service has been good.

6. **The coperto, the cover charge for bread and linens in a restaurant,** can be avoided by going to tavola caldas or pizza-by-the-slice outlets.

7. **The Value Added Tax (or VAT) amounts to up to 19% of your purchases.** Stores in major shopping streets generally offer the VAT Refund program for purchases over a certain amount, usually 300,000 lire. Take your passport and ask the shop to do the paperwork; then follow the instructions to get your refund at the airport.

8. **Just like anywhere, there are sometimes mistakes in bills at restaurants.** Check as you would at home and politely point out any discrepancy to the waiter.

9. **Marked prices** on goods include tax.

10. **Prices in department stores can be more attractive than boutique prices on basic merchandise,** such as underwear, pajamas and the like. Usually there is a better selection and a wider array of sizes.

The Top 10 Ways To Get Around In Rome

Rome is a walking city. Still, public transportation is a good way to go from one section of the city to another. Tickets for public transport (buses, the metro subway, and trams) are available at tobacco stores and some newsstands, as well as from machines located near major bus stops. Each ticket is good for unlimited travel, for a stated length of time, on all forms of public transport. Inside the buses and trams are orange boxes, where tickets must be stamped after boarding. The metro has gates which accept tickets prior to boarding.

1. On foot

There is no way to avoid spending a great deal of time on foot in Rome, so comfortable shoes are a must. Walking is the best way to get a sense of the city. Walking tours can be arranged through services such as Mirabilia Urbis.
Tel. 066832058

2. Regular and Electric buses

Route maps are available from tourist information kiosks. The electric buses are primarily for travel within the centro, the old part of the city. Be careful of pickpockets on all buses.

3. Tour buses

Guided tours are available through travel agents and hotels.

4. Metro

Rome's underground train service doesn't cover the entire city, but it is being expanded.

5. Car

Driving in Rome requires intestinal fortitude, as well as the patience to find a parking space. Small cars are recommended. Park only in authorized parking spaces.

6. Motorino

Renting motorcycles is possible, though negotiating the traffic in Rome is a terrifying prospect for most people.
Roma Scooter Rent Tel 06 6876455
Two Wheels is Better Tel 06 68 77239

7. Bicycle

Bicycles are available for rent and are an excellent way to enjoy the parks and ancient roads, such as the Via Appica Antica.

Rentals in: Piazza di Spagna, Piazza del Popolo, Piazza S. Silvestro, Piazza Augusto Imperatore

8. Taxi

It is difficult to flag down a taxi down on the street; stands are located in major piazzas, or ordered by telephone at 066645, 063570 or 064994. A trip to the airport runs about $50 from the center of the city.

9. Car and driver

Private cars and drivers can be an excellent way to see the city if you are short of time and long on cash. One such service is Europcar Chauffeur Service.

Tel. 0652200147.

10. Trams

The trams (streetcars) are a comfortable way to connect with bus routes and the subway.

A major stop is at Piazza Mancini

Bocca della Venta

The Top 10 Things To Know To Drive In Rome

If you do decide to rent a car, Buona fortuna! This is probably the time to explain about the different police forces. The carabinieri are the military police, though they perform the same function as the regular police force. They wear dark jackets and light blue pants. The regular police, or polizia, wear light blue-gray uniforms. They investigate crimes and make arrests. The Vigili Urbani or traffic police, called the "pizzardone" by the Romans, cannot make arrests. Dressed in black uniforms, they give parking tickets.

1. **Most rental car agencies,** such as Hertz and Avis, have offices in the major hotels.
   Complete list in the English Yellow Pages, www.eypdaily.it

2. **Europcar and Dollaro Express** are also good possibilities.

3. **If you want to explore the center of Rome,** try parking in the underground Villa Borghese parking garage, entered from the Muro Torto road. Take your ticket with you, as you must pay before you pick up your car.

4. **Also near the center is the Via Ludovisi parking garage,** which is near the Via Veneto. Here, you pay as you leave.

5. **There is parking near the Villaggio Olimpico** near the Piazza Mancini, where many bus and tram lines stop.

6. **It is also possible to park on the streets** surrounding the Piazza Mancini. Just be sure to lock your car and hide any valuables, such as cell phones and radios.

7. **Parking spaces** marked with white lines are free.

8. **Parking spaces marked with blue lines** must be paid for in advance. Look for the machine nearby, insert the number of coins required to cover the time you intend to spend. When the ticket comes out of the machine, place it on your dashboard so that it can be seen from the outside.

9. **Scratch off parking passes** can be purchased at tobacccco stores. Scratch off as directed and place on the dashboard of your car so it can be seen from outside.

10. **There is a new parking garage near the Vatican** built for the Jubilee year. It can be reached from the Lungotevere (river road) between the Vatican and Trastevere.

10 More Things To Know About Driving In Rome

1. **When you are stopped at a traffic light,** look carefully before proceding at the green light. Often, there will be a car coming the other way, trying to get through before the light turns red.

2. **At 11 p.m., the traffic lights in Rome** go to yellow blinking lights. Use caution when going through intersections.

3. **Give priority to traffic coming from your right.**

4. **Don't be surprised to find that Roman drivers** have turned a two-lane road into a four-lane or more by squeezing into every available space. Remember, it's every man for himself.

5. **Speed limits are suggestions.**

6. **Seat belts are required by law.**

7. **If you have an accident,** you will need to fill out a Friendly Declaration of Accident form at the scene.
    If you have rented a car, it's better to telephone the rental company before leaving the scene.

8. **Pedestrians have no rights.** Try to avoid them, but it is not necessary to stop for them unless there is a traffic light.

9. **Stop signs are merely a suggestion**; look carefully before proceding.

10. **If your car has disappeared and you think it has been towed,** you must call the Comando dei Vigili Urbani, at 0667691, to find out where it is and to get it back.

The Top 10 Ancient Roman Roads and One New One

It's been said for thousands of years, "All roads lead to Rome," and indeed at one time they did. The Roman Republic (590 BC – 14 BC) was the first to build real roads, naming them after the consuls who decided to build them. These roads ran between Rome and its provinces, making it easier to control them and to move armies where they were needed. Today, these ancient consular roads are still in use - although, of course, they have been upgraded through the centuries. Here's a list of the original Roman roads and where they go. When you find yourself on one of them, think of the history that has passed that way.

1. **Via Aurelia**
   Goes north of Rome to the border of the French Mediterranean Coast. Often used by taxi drivers to go to the airport.

2. **Via Cassia**
   Goes to Viterbo and on to Florence.

3. **Via Flaminia**
   Goes to Terni, Umbria, and the northern Adriatic Coast at Fano.

4. **Via Salaria**
   Goes to Rieti and Abruzzo, on the southern Adriatic.

5. **Via Tiburtina**
   Goes to Tivoli and Avezzano.

6. **Via Prenestina**
   Goes to Palestrina.

7. **Via Casilina**
   Goes to Frosinone.

8. **Via Tuscolana**
   Goes to Castelli Romani.

9. **Via Appia Antica**
   Goes towards Naples on the Mediterranean and on to Brindisi on the Adriatic.

10. **Grande Raccordo Anulare (GRA)**
    A modern road, which is the ring road around the city.

The Top 10 Things To Know About Restrooms In Rome

The public facilities in Italy range from beautifully clean and well stocked to filthy without a working sink. Preparation is the key.

1. **By law, all bars must have public restroom facilities.** However, you should order something, anything, before asking to use the toilette. Otherwise, you may be told the bagno is "guasto," or out of order.

2. **There are very nice public facilities** in the Piazza Risorgimento near the Vatican.

3. **The Vatican Museum** has many clean public restrooms.

4. **The concrete cubicles** seen occasionally on the streets, called vespasiani, are for men only.

5. **Always take toilet paper** and/or tissues with you; seat covers and moistened towelettes can also be useful.

6. **The antibacterial soap gels** popular in the States and now sold in Italy are good to have in purse or pocket as they require no water or paper towels for use.

7. **Sometimes, public restrooms have no seats** on the toilets. Apparently this is for reasons related to cleaning.

8. **Worse, some restrooms have no toilet at all** - only raised ceramics footprints strategically placed near an open drain. Using them can be tricky, requiring good balance; they can be difficult for older people.

9. **Many public restrooms are unisex facilities.** Don't be shocked if someone of the opposite sex comes out of the stall next to yours.

10. **Names in Italian** for the bathroom: toilette, bagno (bahn-yo), gabinetto.

The Top 10 Medically Related Things To Know In Rome

1. **You have a fever** if your temperature is over 37 degrees Centigrade; your temperature is usually taken under the arm in Italy.

2. **Temperature equivalents:** 98.6F (37C) 99.5(37.5) 100.4 (38) 101.3(38.5) 102.2 (39) 103.1 (39.5) 104 (40).

3. **Telephone an ambulance by dialing 113.**

4. **If you have a prescription, carry it with you on your trip to Italy.** Some Roman pharmacists will sell you medicines requiring a prescription in the US if you have the package or bottle to show them.

5. **The American Embassy or Consulate** can provide you with a list of English speaking doctors.

6. **Some hospitals in Italy will accept Blue Cross** Blue Shield; otherwise plan to purchase travel insurance.

7. **Medicare is not accepted** outside the U.S. (remember that at the next election).

8. **To call the Red Cross** (Croce Rossa) in an emergency, dial 5100.

9. **An Emergency Room** or Clinic is signified by the sign, Pronto Soccorso.

10. **The American Hospital in Rome** is located at Via Emilio Longoni, 69, telephone 0625671.

The Top 10 Things To Know When Ordering Food And Drink In Rome

1. **Sitting down doubles the price.** To avoid sticker shock, you should know that to sit at a table at a bar may double the price of your order or more, whether you sit inside or out. The extra charge is to cover the cost of the waiters who serve you. Of course, if you are exhausted from a day of sightseeing, you may be willing to pay for the chair and service. In some few cases, there will be tables and no waiters. Here, you can order at the counter and carry your purchases to sit down.

2. **Look for the cash register.** Before placing your order for a drink or something to eat in a bar where you will be standing or where there are no waiters, it is necessary to pay first for your purchases. Take the receipt to the bar and place your order with the barman.

3. **Il coperto is the cover charge.** Much consternation is caused among visitors to Italy who see on their restaurant bills a charge for something called il coperto. This covers the cost of napkins, bread and other overhead.

4. **Tips, plus.** All bills for food and drink in Italy include a 15% service charge, but most people tip an additional 5-10% in cash when they pay the check.
   At bars in Rome, it is the custom to put a 100 or 200-lire coin on the counter atop the receipt for your order as a tip for the barman. Pay attention to ala carte. Ala carte in Rome means that what is written on the menu is exactly what you get. In other words, if you order beefsteak, you will receive beefsteak and only that on your plate. Anything else must be ordered separately unless the menu specifies otherwise. An order of pasta does not include salad, as it does in many other countries.

6. **Bread is always served in Roman restaurants** - it is included in il coperto. You must ask for butter or olive oil.

7. **In most Roman ristorante,** house wine is very good and very cheap. It can be ordered in several different quantities. Vino rosso is red, vino bianco is white. In Italy, wine is rarely ordered by the glass. The carta dei vini, or wine list, is available for ordering full bottles of specific wines.

8. **Two other important beverages in Rome** are mineral water (acqua minerale) and beer (birra). You must ask for mineral water and indicate whether you would like it gassata (with bubbles) or non gassata or naturale (flat). Birra alla spina is draft beer (usually Italian and very light). Peroni Anastro Azzuro is a local beer which is stronger.

9. **Roman meals are served in a series of courses,** beginning with an optional antipasto and continuing through the primo (pasta, rice or soup), secondo (meat or fish), and ending with dolce (dessert). Accompanying the secondo, diners usually order a contorno (salad, vegetable or both). Portions are not overly large and it is possible to ask for una mezza, or half portion. It is acceptable to delete both the antipasto and dessert, but diners in fine restaurants or trattorias should plan to order both primo and secondo (or pasta with salad and dessert) in order not to seem rude or cheap.

10. **Try fruit for dessert.** Romans often have fruit for dessert instead of heavy sweets. Fruit can be ordered either whole or macedonia (a fresh multi-fruit cocktail). There are some traditional Roman desserts that you should try at least once, including tiramisu, gelati and sorbetti, and torta Romana (ricotta cheese pie).

The Top 10 Differences In Culture And Manners In Rome

Remember the old saying, when in Rome, do as the Romans do.

1. **The biggie: smoking.**
   It's true: more Romans smoke than Americans, and they smoke in public. You will have to deal with it.

2. **Touching and invasion of personal space are natural in Italy,** which has a warm and friendly population. Of course, touching personal spaces isn't to be tolerated, especially on public transportation. Sometimes, however, an Italian will "get in your face" without meaning to offend.

3. **Your mother told you to keep your elbows off the table,** but in Italy it is customary for diners to eat with both hands showing during meals. This goes back in history to the time when your dinner partner might be hiding a weapon in his lap. If he was to be trusted, he had to eat with both hands on the table.

4. **Don't look for a bread plate** unless you are eating in a fine restaurant that caters to foreign tourists. In Italy, bread is placed on the table and never on your plate. It's the way it is, crumbs and all.

5. **The Italians, and other Europeans, eat "backwards,"** from the Americans, never changing their fork from hand to hand. Knives are used to push the food onto the fork. At dessert, expect to use a spoon and fork the same way.

6. **Bella figura,** the image you project, is everything in Italy. Even the most modestly paid shop girls try for a chic appearance. Italians find Americans who travel or sightsee in shorts, t-shirts, leggings and the like to be uncouth.

7. **Hostess gifts are the norm in Italy.**
   If you are invited for dinner, bring your hostess a little gift. Wine is not a good idea, as it might suggest your hosts will not be offering a worthy beverage.

8. **Italians are not bargain hunters.**
   It's one thing to bargain at an outdoor market, but it is offensive to try to bargain in a nice store, although if you buy a lot, you can expect a small discount as a thank you

9. **Italians prefer to dress for breakfast.**
   If you're a houseguest, don't come to the table in your
   pajamas and robe.

10. **When an Italian sneezes,** ignore it. Don't expect him to
    say "Bless you" when you sneeze. That's considered impolite
    as it calls attention to you.

10 More Differences In Culture And Manners

Yes, there are a few more things you should know about Roman culture and manners.

1. **No chrysanthemums, please. In Italy, this flower is reserved for funerals and should never be given as a hostess gift or taken to a hospital.** If you wish to give flowers to your hostess, they will be welcomed. If you know the people well, it's appropriate to take the flowers to the occasion; if not, it's polite to send them prior to the event.

2. **Strikes are a way of life in countries like Italy.** Though sometimes they seem to happen too often, they are never long lasting. Look at them as a minor inconvenience and find another way to travel on that day.

3. **Merchandise returns aren't a way of life in Italy.** If you do try to return something, make sure you have proof of purchase and try to get an exchange rather than a cash refund. If the merchandise is damaged, you may have to argue that it wasn't your fault. In Rome, the customer is not always right.

4. **Driving in Rome** can be terrifying, challenging, frustrating, or fun, depending on your mood and personality. It is especially irritating to try to turn left and find that another car has crept up on your right and suddenly turns left across you. Or, to turn left and face a phalanx of motorcycles coming the wrong way toward you as they try to pass the cars stopped by the stoplight in their own lane. The flip side is that there is really no speed limit and you can park almost anywhere you can squeeze a place, provided you're not in a handicapped zone or walkway.

5. **Ice. Don't ask for it** unless you're willing to deal with one or two pieces. It's considered ridiculous in Rome to take up space in your glass with ice instead of soda. They believe that Americans are regularly cheated in the US when they buy a glass of ice with very little beverage. Many Italians believe that a very cold drink is dangerous to your health if you drink it on a very hot day.

6. **Air conditioners/fans.** Very few Italians have them at home and many hotels have less than adequate cooling systems. If you are desperate, go into a ferramenta (hardware store) and buy a cheap fan for your room. Italians believe that it is bad for your health to sit or sleep with a fan blowing directly on you. A polite restauranteur will turn the fan away from you if you sit too close.

7. **Kissing both cheeks of friends** when you arrive and leave is expected. Kissing only one check is reserved for your spouse or sweetheart. If you don't kiss, be sure to shake hands with everyone upon your arrival and before you depart.

8. **Titles. Unless you are very close to someone,** you must always call them Signora or Signorina - never Signora (Lastname). The thing is, nobody in Italy wants to be just plain Signor. There are lawyers, who should be addressed as Avvocato, professors, who must be called Professore, etc. If you are in doubt, refer to the person as Dottore, a title everyone with a university degree in Italy assumes. When you speak to the waiter or the bus driver, that is the time to use the title, Signor.

9. **Nobility.** With the creation of the Italian Republic after World War II, noble titles legally ceased to exist. But they continue to be used by some in social life and they are everywhere, since titles were given by everybody from the pope to the various kings of the different parts of Italy before unification. When addressing someone with a title, call him barone or conte without using the last name. Sometimes the younger member of a titled family will call himself Don (or Donna for a woman), signaling that they come from a noble family.

10. **Maiden names are generally retained** by Italian women when they marry. Don't automatically call a married woman by her husband's last name, unless she indicates that that is proper.

The Top 10 Hand Gestures In Rome

Italians are known for their detailed hand gestures. You may want to avoid using hand gestures when speaking to an Italian in case you are misunderstood. Still, it's fun, and useful, to know what they mean.

1. **When an Italian wants you to come to him**, he will make a gesture that looks to an American or Englishman as if he wants you to go away. He turns his palm to the ground and wags his fingers back and forth.

2. **When an Italian is counting,** he uses his thumb for number one, followed by the other fingers.

3. **Raising the forefinger** and pinkie with the fingers pointed to the ground means "good luck," or "knock on wood." Pointing the fingers upwards or toward someone means "you are a cuckold."

4. **Extending the thumb** and first two fingers and twisting your wrist indicates you are interested in eating pasta. The gesture is similar to the fork that twists the pasta up from your plate.

5. **Hitting the palm of the left hand** perpendicularly with the side of the other hand, fingers point outwards on both hands, means, "Go away!"

6. **Pulling down the bottom** eyelid means "pay attention."

7. **Hitting the hipbone** with the outside edge of the open hand means "I'm hungry."

8. **Writing in the** air tells the waiter to "bring the check."

9. **Hitting the extended forefingers** of both hands together to make a kind of scissors means "together," sometimes used to indicate two people are having an affair.

10. **Making a pistol of the hand** and twisting it back and forth means you opinion is negative.

Top 10 Phone Numbers To Know While Visiting Rome

1. **AT&T OPERATOR** 172 1011
2. **MCI OPERATOR** 172 1022
3. **SPRINT OPERATOR** 172 1877
4. **ITALIAN DIRECTORY ASSISTANCE** 12
5. **INTERNATIONAL DIRECTORY ASSISTANCE** 176
6. **INTERNATIONAL OPERATOR** 170
7. **TIME** 161
8. **STATE POLICE** 113
9. **CARABINIERI (MILITARY POLICE)** 112
10. **FIRE** 115

The Top 10 Places To Find Tourist Information

1. **Octagonal green kiosks**
   Located around Rome and staffed with English speaking information officers.
   A very convenient one is near the intersection of Via Corso at the opposite end of Via Condotti from the Spanish Steps.

2. **The Termini**
   Has an excellent information booth.
   Main train station

3. **Leonardo da Vinci Airport, a.k.a. Fiumicino**
   Has tourist information in each terminal.

4. **Near Castel Sant'angelo, a.k.a. Hadrian's Tomb**
   On the river near the Vatican.

5. **On Via Nazionale**
   Near the Piazza Repubblica.

6. **"Where"**
   A publication available at various newsstands.

7. **"Wanted in Rome"**
   The bi-weekly magazine available at English bookstores and newsstands, is an excellent source of information.

8. **"Time Out"**
   Roman edition, sold at newsstands

9. **"English Yellow Pages"**
   Sold in bookshops.
   Updates at www.eypdaily.it

10. **Roman Call Center**
    English-speaking operators are standing by to answer questions and provide information.
    Tel. 06 3600 4399.

The Top 10 Things To Know About Dating

1. **When a woman is accosted on the street** by a flirtatious man, she should ignore him completely, walk straight on and say nothing; otherwise, he will think she is interested.

2. **Italian men** want and expect to pay for their dates.

3. **Italian women** expect the man to pay.

4. **Sex is not expected** on the first date.

5. **A normal first date** can be a stroll through the city followed by a pizza.

6. **Often, the man waits in the street for the woman without knocking on her door**, or they arrange to meet somewhere, such at a piazza or a fountain.

7. **Italians don't like drunks**, so it is important not to over imbibe.

8. **Men should not push for sex**; it is much better to be circumspect and patient.

9. **Dress on a first date is casual** unless circumstances require otherwise.

10. **Italian women** expect men to telephone them.

The Top 10 Things For Animal Lovers To Know

1. **Italians love animals** and often can be seen feeding strays on the street.

2. **Rome is famous for its feral cats,** particularly those that inhabit ancient ruins.

3. **Guided tours are available** to visit historical sites "where emperors ruled and now cats reign," by calling 065756085 or 063217951.

4. **Cats are so loved in Rome** that there are special calendars sold at souvenir kiosks that feature photos of cats and ancient ruins.

5. **Often there will be cats wandering around** outdoor cafes. If you want to, feed them. If you don't, then ignore them and they will visit another table.

6. **Rome has a very nice zoo,** located on the Viale del Giardino Zoologico 20.

7. **The she-wolf** is the symbol of the city . Statues of the she-wolf and her adopted babies, Romulos and Remus, can be seen throughout the city.

8. **The obelisk in Piazza della Minerva** is a Bernini sculpture featuring an elephant.

9. **Turtles are celebrated** in the design of the Fontana delle Tartarughe, a fountain built in the piazza Mattei in 1581.

10. **The majestic lions surrounding** the ancient obelisk in piazza del Popolo were sculpted of marble in the 19th century.

The Top 10 English Speaking Associations In Rome

1. **American Club**
   Tel. 063295843

2. **American Women's Association**
   Tel. 064825268

3. **Canadian Women's Association**
   Tel. 069088050

4. **Commonwealth Club**
   Tel. 0685303005

5. **International Women's Club of Rome**
   Tel. 0633267490

6. **Navy League of the United States**
   Tel. 065828519

7. **Professional Women's Association**
   Tel. 0685303487

8. **United Nations Women's Guild**
   Tel. 0657056503

9. **Welcome Neighbor**
   Tel. 0630366936

10. **Caritas Foreigners' Support Center**
    Tel. 066875228

The Top 10 Most Important Signs You Will See

1. **The white capital "T"** on a dark background indicates a store that sells stamps, parking tickets, bus tickets and the like.

2. **A capital "M"** indicates a Metro station.

3. **The word Fermata** indicates a bus station. Route numbers are listed below. Capolinea is the end of the line.

4. **Senso unico** indicates a one-way street.

5. **Sosta vietata** written on a circular blue and red sign indicates no parking.

6. **A small letter "i"** indicates an information booth for tourists.

7. **A capital "H"** indicates hospital.

8. **Taxi stands** are indicated by blue signs with the word taxi.

9. **A white triangular sign with a red frame** indicates the driver is to yield.

10. **A round sign with a drawing of a telephone receiver** indicates a public phone.

The Top 10 English Language Theatre And Movies In Rome

1. **Alcazar**
   English films on Monday.
   Via Merry del Val 14

2. **Intrastevere**
   Films in original language when available.
   Vicolo Moroni 3A

3. **Nuovo Sacher**
   Films in original language on Monday.
   Largo Ascianghi 1

4. **Pasquino**
   Films in English every day.
   Piazza S. Egidio 10

5. **Quirinetta**
   Films in original language everyday.
   Via Minghetti 4

6. **Warner Village**
   In English, Monday and Tuesday.
   Parco de' Medici, Magliana

7. **Off Night Repertory Theater**
   In English, October through June. "Friday Night Live"

8. **Centro Gropius**
   Will provide interpreters in English.
   Via S. Telesforo 7

9. **The Abbey Theatre (music)**
   Via del Governo Vecchio 51/53

10. **Palazzo delle Esposizioni**
    Shows series of international films.
    Via Milano 9A

The Top 10 Italian Language Schools In Rome

1. **Berlitz**
    Via di Torre Argentina 21
    Tel 066834000

2. **Centro Studi Cassia**
    Via Sesto Miglio 16
    Tel 0633253852

3. **Studioitalia**
    Via Tibullo 10
    Tel 0668307796

4. **Italiaidea**
    Piazza della Cancelleria 85
    Tel 066892997

5. **Centro Studi Flaminio**
    Via Flaminia 21
    Tel 063610903

6. **Dilit**
    Via Marghera 22
    Tel 0644626202

7. **Lead On**
    Via Cannizzaro 51
    Tel 0640802030

8. **Villa Borghese**
    Via Sicilia 125
    Tel 0642012537

9. **Torre di Babele**
    Via Bixio 74
    Tel 067008434

10. **Mediterraneo**
    Via Genova 30
    Tel 064747955

The Top 10 Web Sites With Information About Rome

1. **www.webguiderome.com/**
   overall guide

2. **www.stockton.edu/ roman/fiction/index.htm**
   fiction written about ancient Rome

3. **members.xoom.com/romeartlover/index.html**
   art

4. **www.mrdowling.com/702rome.html**
   general

5. **www.b-b.rm.it/**
   bed and breakfasts

6. **www.catacombe.roma.it/indice_fr.html**
   catacombs

7. **www.enjoyrome.com/**
   tourist office site

8. **pub.xplore.it/nerone/hp.htm**
   insider's guide

9. **www.romeguide.it/**
   general

10. **www.eypdaily.it**
    English Yellow Pages

The Top 10 Artistic Events In Rome

The best ways to get updated information on these events are through the green tourist kiosks, in Wanted in Rome or Where magazines, or in Trova Roma, a weekly publication in Italian.

1. **Art Fair**
   Spring and Fall; held in one of Rome's most beautiful old streets, this fair is more for browsing than buying, as the prices are high, but it's well worth the trip.
   Via Margutta

2. **Antique Furniture Week (Fiera dell'Antiquariato)**
   Second half of May; beautiful at night when the ancient streets are lit by torches; very expensive, but worth a visit.
   Via dei Coronari

3. **The Rose Show**
   May and June; wondrous flowers.
   Garden of Via di Valle Murcia

4. **Annual Art Exhibition**
   May/June.
   American Academy in Rome

5. **Crafts Fair**
   October; antiques, leatherwork, jewellery and gifts.
   Via dell' Orso

6. **Natale Oggi**
   June. Special Italian Christmas gifts.
   EUR district, Fiera di Roma

7. **Spanish Steps Alta Moda Fashion Show**
   July; only VIPs gets seats to this glamourous event, but others can watch from the piazza.
   Spanish Steps and Piazza di Spagna

8. **Flower Festival**
   June, the streets are paved with flowers.
   In the town of Genzano

9. **Opera**
   Concerts and drama outdoors. July/August.

10. **Roma Jazz Festival**
    July.

The Top 10 Plus Two Public Holidays In Rome

The Vatican declares many more holidays and saints days than these, which can affect the opening hours of the Vatican museum. This list names official government-ordained public holidays when most shops, banks and government offices and facilities are closed. April 21, the birthday of Rome, is not a public holiday; it is called a day of National Solemnity.

1. **January 1,** New Year's Day

2. **January 6**, Epiphany

3. **Easter Monday**

4. **April 25**, Liberation from Nazi Fascism

5. **May 1**, Labor Day

6. **June 2**, Republic Day

7. **June 29,** Saints Peter and Paul, holiday only in Rome

8. **August 15**, Ferragosto mid-summer holiday

9. **November 1**, All Saints Day

10. **December 8**, Immaculate Conception

11. **December 25**, Christmas

12. **December 26**, Saint Stephen's Day

The Top 10 Calendar Events In Rome

On these days, almost everything will be closed.

1. 6 January, Epiphany

The feast of Befana, the witch who predated Santa Claus in Italy and brings gifts to good children. The center of activity during this holiday season is Piazza Navona. Kiosks filled with toys take over the square. Most businesses are closed.

2. Carnevale

Marked in Rome by costume parties, store decorations, special sugary pastries (frappe) baked for the season. Carnevale corresponds with Mardi Gras.

3. Holy Week

The week surrounding Easter is a collection of major holiday in Rome. The Pope holds masses throughout the city and there are processions on Good Friday. The Monday after Easter is a public holiday.

4. March 8 - International Women's Day

Every woman is given yellow mimosas. Some restaurants have special meals just for their female customers, where mimosas decorate the tables.

5. International Horse Show

Held in late Spring, this event is the focal point for horse lovers from all over the world.

6. Antique Furniture Week

Held in May, antique dealers are crowded with customers and antiques fairs are held along the riverbanks. Some good buys, as well as some excellent fakes, are available for purchase.

7. Feast of Sts. Peter and Paul, June 29

Celebration to honor the patron saints of Rome.

8. Summer Festival.

Held along the Tiber River. Every evening the program features music, food, dancing, and other activities.

9. 15 August, Ferragosto.

Dating back over two thousand years, this end of summer holiday finds most Romans at the beach. Don't expect anything to be open on Ferragosto.

10. Feast of the Immaculate Conception - December 8.

This is a public holiday and everything is closed.

The Top 10 Festivals In Rome

1. **Epiphany,** Sunday preceding the 6 of January. The grand finale of the marvelous toy fair in Piazza Navona.

2. **Carnival**, from Epiphany until the beginning of Lent.

3. **The Feast of St. Joseph,** 19 March. Sweets are sold in the streets.
   Trionfale district

4. **Easter**, Holy Week through Easter Monday. There are rites and religious functions around the city.

5. **Spring Festival In April.** Piazza di Spagna is covered in azaleas

6. **The Feast of St. John**, 23-24 June. Stewed snails and roast suckling pig.

7. **The Feast of Noantri**, mid-July. Food and fireworks, great fun.
   Trastevere

8. **Summer Festival** - July and August. Throughout the city, multiple events and concerts

9. **Ferragosto**, 15 August. Everyone goes to the country, so you can try plenty of parking, though many restaurants are closed.

10. **Feast of the Immaculate Conception**, 8 December.
    In Piazza di Spagna, fireman climb a ladder to place a wreath of flowers on the head of the Madonna statue atop the column.

Michelangelo's *Moses*

Dining In Rome

The Top 10 Restaurants In Rome

1. La Pergola, Rome Hilton Cavalieri
The best restaurant in Rome, where the view competes with the menu. Both are spectacular. The wine cellar is home to 1350 labels.
Via A. Cadlolo, 101, Tel. 0635092211

2. 'Gusto
A sensation since its opening in 1998. Young chef, old wines.
Piazza Augusto Imperatore 9, Tel. 06 3226273

3. Hassler Roof Garden
Not only is the view spectacular, but the food is excellent, though not exactly typically Roman. Very expensive, top quality service, good wine list.
Piazza Trinita' dei Monti, 6, in the Hotel Hassler Villa Medici, Tel.06699340

4. La Terrazza dell' Eden, Eden Hotel
Some say that this restaurant, which has served the royal court of England, was once the best in Rome. Still has an excellent wine list, divine desserts, sensational view.
Via Ludovisi, 49, Tel. 0647812552

5. Le Sans Souci
Homey atmosphere, excellent service, wonderful food.
Via Sicilia 24, Tel. 064821814

6. Agata and Romeo
Less touristy than the hotel restaurants, this top notch kitchen offers Roman specialities prepared with creativity mixed with tradition.
Via Carlo Alberto, 45, Tel 064466115

7. Papa Baccus
Traditional Tuscan, excellent fresh fish.
Via Toscana, 36, Tel. 0642742808

8. Pauline Borghese de L'hotel Parco dei Principi
Excellent chef, elegant setting.
Via G.B. Pergolesi 2, Tel 06854421

9. Margutta Vegetariano

It's easy to forget this restaurant is vegetarian - the menu is a delight of tastes and freshness. Billing itself as a "Ristorarte," Margutta feeds the soul with regular art exhibits.
Piazza Rondanini, 53, Tel. 0668134544

10. Jeff Blynn's

Beautiful setting, sushi bar and Sunday brunch.
Viale Parioli 103/c, Tel: 068070444

Trevi Fountain

10 More Top Restaurants In Rome

1. Da Pancrazio

If you want to eat with history, this is the place. The site is the ancient theater of Pompey, where Caesar was reputedly stabbed to death. Comprehensive wine list, typical Roman table, and an underground dining room reeking with history.
Piazza del Discione, 92/94, Tel. 066861246

2. George's

Lovely atmosphere, nice food.
Via Marche 7, Tel. 06 42084575

3. La Rosetta

Imaginative menu, excellent food, including top quality shellfish.
Via della Rosetta 9, Tel. 066861002

4. Ai Tre Scalini

Limited seating, cosy and intimate, outstanding menu.
Via del SS. Quattro 30, Tel. 067096309

5. Vecchia Roma

Located in a secluded piazza, it's wonderful in summer.
Piazza Campitelli 18, Tel. 066864604

6. La Veranda de L'Hotel Majestic

Beautiful setting, good service, wide-ranging menu.
Via Vittorio Veneto 50, Tel. 06486841

7. Alberto Ciarla

A very good seafood restaurant with excellent service.
Piazza S. Cosimato 40, Tel. 065818668

8. Antico Arco

Longtime success comes from unpretentious excellence.
Piazzale Aurelio 7, Tel. 065815274

9. Da Piperno

The dessert specialty, palle del nonno (Grandpa's balls), adds spice to this evocative old restaurants located in the ancient Jewish Ghetto. Offerings include the famous Jewish-style artichokes, baccala, and fiori fritti.
Monte de' Cenci 9, Tel. 0668806629

10. Camponeschi

Beautiful setting with the beautiful people, good food.
Piazza Farnese 50, Tel. 066874927

The Top 10 Late Night Restaurants In Rome

Late night dining in Rome usually means after-theatre.

1. **Alberto Ciarla**
   Open late all year, full menu.
   Piazza S. Cosimato, 40, Trastevere, Tel 06 5818668

2. **Antico Bottaro**
   Closed Mondays and August.
   Passeggiata di Ripetta, Centro Storico, Tel 06 3236763

3. **Camponeschi**
   Closed Sunday except for evenings and in August.
   Campo de' Fiori, Tel 06 6874927

4. **Ciccia Bomba**
   Closed Wednesdays and in August, good menu.
   Via del Governo Vecchio, 76, Piazza Navona, Tel 06 68802108

5. **Due Ladroni**
   Good food, open 'til dawn.
   Piazza Nicosia 24, Tel 06 6861013

6. **Edy**
   Closed Sundays in August, intimate and simple.
   Vialo del Babuino,4, Piazza Popolo, Tel 06 36001738

7. **'Gusto**
   Closed Mondays, booking necessary.
   Piazza Augusto, Centro Storico, Tel 06 3226273

8. **Harry's Bar**
   Closed Sundays and some holidays. La Dolce Vita preserved.
   Via Veneto, 150, Tel 06 484643

9. **La Ninfa de L'Hotel Majestic**
   Open 7 days a week, 365 days a year, until 1 a.m.
   Via Vittorio Veneto, 54, Tel 06 42010693

10. **Rosati Due**
    A neighborhood hangout, call first for hours.
    Piazzale Clodio, Tel. 06383889

Top 10 Places To Eat With A View Of Rome

1. Castel Sant'Angelo Snack Bar

A more casual location and a wonderful place to break from a day of sightseeing. The food is good and the view is stupendous.

Lungotevere Castello near the Vatican

2. The Hassler Roof Restaurant, Hassler Hotel.

This restaurant is an elegant eaterie. Very expensive, very beautiful, very romantic. A gorgeous view of the city from its perch atop the Spanish Steps.

Piazza Trinita dei Monti, 6. Tel 06 6782651

3. The Forum Hotel.

Its sunny rooftop terrace offers wonderful views of the Forum and Colosseum.

Via Tor di Conti, 25,
Tel. 06 6792446

4. La Pergola at The Cavalieri Hilton.

With its panoramic view of the city, this restaurant has been declared the best in Rome. Save this one for a special night out. Unless you are staying at the Hilton, on the Monte Mario Hill, you will need to take a taxi.

Via A. Cadlolo,101,
Tel. 06 35091

5. La Terrazza at The Eden Hotel.

If it's a view you are looking for, this is one of the best in the center of Rome. La Terazza is a place for a lovely, and expensive, evening out.

Via Ludovisi, 49,
Tel. 06 47812752

6. The Domus Aventina Hotel bar.

Located on the Aventine Hill in a restored convent, the hotel overlooks the church of Santa Prisca. A quiet, serene setting. Drop in after a long day of sightseeing.

Via di Santa Prisca 11B,
Tel. 06 5746135

7. The Piazzale Garibaldi trattorias.

Up on the Janiculum Hill, where the puppet shows reign, the trattorias and coffee bars that overlook the city are pleasant places to stop for a drink or a snack.

8. The Capitolini Museum Café.

It's nice to know there is a museum café that offers food for hungry visitors, as well as food for their souls with its wonderful view of old Rome.
Piazza Campodoglio

9. Zodiaco bar, Monte Mario.

Can't afford the Cavalieri Hilton, but want a similar view from Monte Mario? Go to the Zodiaco bar near the intersection of Viale Trianfale and the Panoramica road. It's a romantic late night spot for a final drink before calling it a night.

10. The Minerva Hotel (Holiday Inn Crowne Plaza)

Views from its roof terrace restaurant/bar include the Pantheon, St. Peter's and the Janiculum hill.
Piazza della Minerva, 69, Tel. 06 6841888

Arch of Titus, Roman Forum

The Top 10 Sidewalk Cafes, Coffee Bars, and Restaurants

What can be more romantic than sitting with a cappuccino at the sunlit tables of an outdoor cafe, overlooking a Roman piazza? Sounds great, as long as you know the score. Sitting outside at a cafe in Rome will double or triple the price of your order.

1. Tre Scallni

Piazza Navona and Tre Scalini go together, along with the decadent ice cream dessert invented there, the chocolate tartufo. Of course, there is also the summer favorite, granita di caffe (a kind of coffee snowcone with whipped cream), cappucino, even food.
Piazza Navona

2. Canova.

Overlooking Piazza del Popolo, the Canova is a wonderful spot for people watching and a favorite hangout for movie stars. A hidden secret, the tavola calda (hot table or cafeteria) in the back offers a good, inexpensive lunch and tables both inside and in a central atrium.
Piazza del Popolo.

3. Rosati.

Across the Piazza del Popolo from Canova, Rosati is where the literary types go to drink their coffee. Equally as interesting a view as Canova's, depending upon the time of day and angle of the sun.
Piazza del Popolo

4. McDonalds's at Piazza della Rotonda.

It sounds crazy, but the McDonald's across the piazza from the Pantheon offers both American comfort food and an incredible view of one of Rome's most interesting sites.
Piazza della Rotonda

5. Carbonara.

There are many ristoranti and bars in the Campo de' Fiori. This one combines good food and a wonderful view of Rome's most colorful outdoor market.
Campo de'Fiori

6. Babington's Tea Rooms.

There's not a lot of choice when it comes to outdoor eating in Piazza di Spagna; in fact, this place only puts tables out in the summer. It's ridiculously expensive, but you can't beat the scenery or atmosphere unless you sit on the Spanish Steps with a can of Coke.

Piazza di Spagna

7. Piazza Santa Maria in Trastevere.

There are many trattorias and bars lining the Piazza Santa Maria in Trastevere - take your pick. You can't go wrong with an order of cappucino, fresh fruit juice, or gelato. The point is to absorb the atmosphere of one of Rome's most ancient neighborhoods.

Piazza Santa Maria in Trastevere

8. CuCuRuCu.

There are only a couple of ristoranti in Rome that sit alongside the Tiber River. This elderly ristorante offers warm ambience inside and tables right on the river in the summer. Between the front door and the patio, diners pass displays of fresh, whole seafood and meats, as well as one of the best antipasto tables in the city.

Just off the Lungotevere near the Piazza Maresciallo Giardino

9. Vecchia Roma.

Set in medieval surroundings behind the Teatro di Marcello, this delightful ristorante offers good food in a splendid setting.

Piazza Campitelli 18
Tel. 066864604

10. Via Veneto.

Along the Via Veneto, between the Porta Pinciana and the American Embassy, there are many coffee bars and ristoranti with sidewalk tables. The prices are usually high, but this area brings back the old days of La Dolce Vita.

The Top 10 Best Coffee Bars In Rome

"Bar" is used to denote an establishment where people drink coffee, tea, apertivos, or soft drinks usually standing up. Pastry, ice cream, and sandwiches are usually offered as well. Italians drop into bars 2 or 3 times a day for a quick coffee. Bars are traditionally open six days a week, from 7 a.m. to 1 a.m. Every bar selects its own day to close.

1. **Caffé Greco**
   Centuries old and elegant, with tables in the back.
   Via Condotti 86

2. **Sant'Eustachio**
   Famous for the quality of its coffee.
   Piazza Sant'Eustachio 82

3. **Tazza d'Oro**
   Known for quality, near the Pantheon.
   Via degli Orfani 82/84

4. **Ristoro della Salute**
   Convenient place to stop after visiting the Colosseum.
   Piazza del Colosseo 2

5. **Vanni**
   Full restaurant and bar, traditional hangout for television crowd, open late.
   Via Col di Lana 10, Via Frattina 94

6. **Giolitti**
   Lovely setting, great pastry.
   Via Uffici del Vicario 40

7. **Ciampini**
   Good place to go in a lovely piazza.
   Piazza S. Lorenzo in Lucina

8. **Antico Caffe della Pace**
   Good place near Piazza Navona.
   Via della Pace 5

9. **Selarum**
   Coffee, as well as late night drinks, in Trastevere.
   Via del Fienaroli 12

10. **Le Caffettiera**
    Restored setting near the Pantheon.
    Piazza di Pietra 65

The Top 10 Pubs

Irish pubs have become popular in Rome and these are the best of the genre, with music and beer at all of them.

1. **Druid's Den**
   Via S. Martino ai Monti 28

2. **Finnegan Pub**
   Via Leonina 66/67

3. **Fiddler's Elbow**
   Via dell'Olmata 43

4. **Four XXXX Pub**
   Via Galvani 29

5. **Miscellanea**
   Via delle Paste 110

6. **O'Connor's Pub**
   Via dei Cartari 7

7. **Shamrock Pub**
   Via Capo d'Africa 26

8. **St. Andrew's Pub**
   Vicolo della Cancelleria 36

9. **Tre Scalini Bistro**
   Via Panisperna 251

10. **Blob**
    Via degli Scipioni 96

The Top 10 Best Wine Bars In Rome

1. **L'Angolo Divino**
   Relatively new, this wine bar has a broad range, from affordable to expensive prices; wonderful appetizers and desserts.
   Via dei Balestrari 12, near Campo de'Fiori

2. **La Bottega del Vino di Anacleto Bleve**
   One of Rome's best stocked wine bars, it also offers great food.
   Via S. Maria del Pianto, 9/11, near the Ghetto

3. **Il Brillo Parlante**
   Crowded and noisy with a good selection of wines.
   Via della Fontanella 12, near Piazza del Popolo

4. **Semidivino**
   A good place for wine lovers. Good food.
   Via Alessandria 230, Pinciano

5. **Tramonti e Muffati**
   Great wine list, interesting. Good food.
   Via Santa Maria Ausiliatrice 105

6. **Trimani Il Wine Bar**
   A Roman institution for the discriminating wine drinker.
   Via Cenaia 37/b, near Termini

7. **Vinamore**
   Relax here after a long day of sightseeing; light snack.
   Via Monte Giordano 63, near Piazza Navona

8. **Alla Corte del Vino**
   More than 200 wines accompanied by a wide choice of appetizers and desserts.
   Via Monte della Farina 43, near Campo de' Fiori

9. **Cul de Sac**
   Fantastic wine list and a menu to match
   Piazza Pasquino 73, near Piazza Navona

10. **Achilli al Parlamento**
    Traditional mescita, wine and champagne, tasting by the glass.
    Via dei Prefetti 15, near the Pantheon

The Top 10 Places To Eat American And International Foods In Rome

1. T Bone Station
Good, traditional steaks and burgers.
Via F. Crispi 25 and Via Flaminia 525/527 at Corso di Francia

2. Hard Rock Café
American food – burgers, fried chicken.
Via V. Veneto 62A

3. Planet Hollywood
American menu with salads, burgers.
Via del Tritone 118

4. Maharajah Indian Restaurant
Indian curries and tandoori.
Via dei Serpenti 124

5. Crazy Bull Café
Burgers and beer.
Via Mantova 5

6. Oliphant Rome
Tex-Mex.
Via delle Coppelle 31/32

7. ATM Sushi Bar
Japanese sushi.
Via della Penitenza 7

8. Jasmine
Traditional Chinese.
Via Sicilia 47

9. Sawasdee
Thai food.
Via le XXI Aprile 13/c

10. Thien Kim
Vietnamese food.
Via Giulia 201

The Top 10 Trattorias And Moderately Priced Restaurants In Rome

Roman trattorias are more casual and moderately priced than restaurants. They are preferred by locals.

1. Augusto

Roman dishes in a family-style atmosphere.
Piazza de' Renzi 15, Trastevere

2. Arancia Blu

A vegetarian restaurant with wonderful food.
Via dei Latini 65

3. Ciccia Bomba

Homemade gnocchi on Thursdays and octopus soup on Fridays. Traditional menu and even wood-fired pizza in the evenings.
Via del Governo Vecchio 76, near Piazza Navona

4. Edy

Wonderful home-style food in one of the city's most expensive neighborhoods.
Via del Babuino 4, historic center

5. Enoteca Corsi

Affordable prices, good food, always crowded.
Via del Gesu' 87/88, historic center

6. Fauro

Wonderful fish.
Via R. Fauro 44, Parioli

7. Hostaria da Zi Adele al Farinone

Great selection of pastas in this typical Roman restaurant.
Via del Farinone 34, near the American Academy

8. Taverna Giulia

Ancient dining rooms, discreet service, yummy food.
Vicolo dell'Oro 23, near Campo de' Fiori

9. Trattoria Monti

Unpretentious with creative cuisine from Le Marche.
Via di San Vito 13A

10. Lo Sgobbone

Family-style with excellent Roman food.
Via dei Podesti 8/10, Flaminio

The Top 10 Of The Thousands Of Pizzerias In Rome

For those accustomed to eating their pizza with pepperoni, take note: in Italian, the word pepperoni means green pepper. If you're a fan of the sausage known as pepperoni, you must order your pizza with salami. Most Roman pizzas are thin crust; Neopolitan pizza has thick crust.

1. Pizza Re

A local favorite, these restaurants serve Neopolitan-style pizza, with thicker crust.
Via di Ripetta 14

2. Acchiappafantasmi

Good traditional pizza with some southern Italian touches.
Via dei Cappellari 66, near Campo de' Fiori

3. La Belle Epoque

Delicious Neopolitan pizza and good desserts.
Via Ajaccio 11

4. Candido

Wood-fired baking and affordable prices.
Viale Angelico 275

5. Di Pietro

Wood-fired baking and good crunchy pizzas.
Piazza di Porta San Paolo 6

6. Est! Est! Est!

Offering both Roman and Neopolitan pizzas since 1905.
Via Genova 32

7. Le Montecarlo

Excellent pizza, be ready for a long wait.
Vicolo Savelli 12

8. Il Regno di Napoli

Neopolitan pizza in the heart of Rome.
Via Romagna 20

9. Remo

The most famous pizzeria in Testaccio.
Piazza S. Maria Libertrice 44

10. La Maremma

Classical pizza of both schools
Viale Parioli 93/c
Via Alessandria 119/d

The Top 10 Best Ice Cream Stores (Gelaterie) In Rome

There is probably no place in Rome that has bad gelato, but here are the very best.

1. Il Gelato di S. Crispino

Try the gelato made with honey from Sardinia.
Via della Panetteria 42

2. Fonte della Salute

Fresh fruit and soy-based ice cream and yogurt.
Via Cardinal Marmaggi 246

3. Yogobar

Features a mascarpone-based cream eaten with yogurt and fruit.
Viale Regina Margherita 83/b

4. Le Procope

Popular with those in the know.
Piazza dei Re di Roma 39, Corso del Rinascimento 58/60, and Via di Conca d'Oro 343

5. Tre Scalini

Order a delectable chocolate tartufo and enjoy the setting, the music, and the ice cream.
Piazza Navona

6. Giolitti

A lovely setting near Parliament; very good ice cream.
Via Uffici del Vacario 40 and in EUR

7. Gelateria della Parma

Fresh and delicious, near the Pantheon.
Via della Maddalena 20

8. Chalet del Lago

Sit beside the lake, day or night, and enjoy.
Casina dei Tre Laghi, Viale Oceania 90, EUR

9. Minim's de Paris

Near the Spanish Steps.
Via di Propaganda 26A

10. Palazzo del Freddo di Giovanni Fassi

Opened in 1924, these gelaterie are strongly traditional.
Via Vespasiano, 56 (Prati), via Principe Eugenio, 65/67 (Esquilino)

The Top 10 Ways To Drink Coffee In Rome

Italians are the most devout coffee drinkers in the world, and have invented many ways to drink this luxurious beverage. A Roman would never touch a cappuccino after 11 a.m.; that's why tourists get the strange looks from waiters when they ask for cappucino after dinner.

1. **Caffe**
   Espresso, very strong aromatic coffee served in a very small cup.

2. **Caffe lungo**
   Espresso diluted with a little water.

3. **Caffe macciato**
   Espresso with a few drops of milk.

4. **Caffe corretto**
   Espresso with grappa, brandy, or Sambuca added.

5. **Caffe americano**
   American coffee.

6. **Caffe latte**
   Espresso with steamed milk with little foam.

7. **Caffe freddo**
   Iced coffee, always served with sugar.

8. **Cappucino**
   Espresso with foamy steamed milk.

9. **Granita di caffe**
   Shaved frozen coffee served with whipped cream and a spoon, found in summer.

10. **Cappucino freddo**
    Iced cappuccino, served sweet.

The Top 10 Pizza By The Slice And Quick Snacks

Pizza by the slice is not really a cuisine; it's more a convenience. Along with the other fast food outlets mentioned on this list, pizza by the slice will help you go on sightseeing!

1. **AP-Pizza Art**
   Via Fonteiana 63, Monteverde Nuovo

2. **Indian Fast Food**
   Via Mamiani 11, Esquiline

3. **Palombini**
   Piazza Adenauer 12, EUR

4. **Le Piramidi**
   Middle Eastern snacks.
   Vicolo del Gallo 11, Campo de' Fiori

5. **Rosticceria**
   Via Famogosta 18, Trionfale

6. **Vanni**
   Via Col di Lana 10, Prati

7. **Zi Fenizia**
   Via S. Marla del Pianto 64/65, Ghetto

8. **Volpetti Piu'**
   Via A. Volta 8, Testaccio

9. **Tornatora**
   Viale della Grande Muraglia 100, EUR

10. **Fonclea**
    Via Crescenzio 82A, Prati

The Top 10 Red Wines To Drink While In Rome

Though some red wine is made locally, it is generally sold by the liter and not by the bottle. Most Romans drink red wine from all around Italy.

1. **Chianti/Chianti Classico** *Tuscany*

2. **Brunello di Montalcino** *Tuscany*

3. **Montefalco Rosso** *Umbria*

4. **Sagrantino di Montefalco** *Umbria*

5. **Vino Nobile di Montepulciano** *Tuscany*

6. **Barolo** *Piedmont*

7. **Barbaresco** *Piedmont*

8. **Corvo Red Wine** *Sicily*

9. **Sassicaia** *Tuscany*

10. **Valpolicella** *Veneto*

Remus, Romulus and the She-Wolf

The Top 10 White Wines To Drink In Rome

The availability of several kinds of locally produced white wines practically ensures that the house wine will be good. Don't hesitate to drink wine served in a pitcher or by the glass.

1. **Frascati**

   A local and very good wine, famous around the world.

2. **Castelli Romani**

   These wines, including the four that follow, are from the Lazio or Rome region, and are usually served in a carafe as a house wine.

3. **Colli Albani**

4. **Fontana Candida**

5. **Marino**

6. **Velletri**

7. **Frizzantino**

   This fizzy wine is served refreshingly cold in summer.

8. **Olevano**

   A local wine.

9. **Orvieto Classico**

   From the medieval Umbrian town of Orvieto, this wine is excellent.

10. **Est, Est, Est di Montefiascone**

    More of a dessert wine, the name comes from an old story: Long ago, a cardinal sent his scouts out ahead of him to look for good wines. If they found one, they marked "Est" ("here" in Latin) on the side of the winery. The story goes that the cardinal's man found a wine he liked so much that he marked "Est, Est, Est" (here, here, here) on the building, a designation which remains to this day.

The Top 10 Food Specialties To Eat In Rome

1. **Fiori di zucca fritti** - deep fried pumpkin or zucchini flowers stuffed with mozzarella and anchovies.

2. **Carciofi alla Romana** - artichokes cooked so tender you can eat everything, even the stem.

3. **Carciofi alla Giudia** - tender artichokes deep fried in the Jewish way.

4. **Crostata di ricotta** - a torte or pie made with fresh ricotta cheese.

5. **Suppli** - deep fried rice balls.

6. **Filetti di baccala** - deep fried filets of codfish, a traditional Jewish dish.

7. **Bucatini alla Matriciana** - a long hollow pasta cooked with a tomato and bacon sauce.

8. **Pasta al Carbonara** - a pasta cooked with eggs and bacon in a creamy sauce.

9. **Pajata** - the milk-filled intestines of a calf slaughtered for veal.

10. **Coda alla vaccinara** - oxtail.

The Second Top 10 Roman Specialty Foods

1. **Abbacchio** - spring lamb roasted in herbs, particularly rosemary.

2. **Porchetta** - pork roasted in a special way and eaten cold; sold from outdoor stands.

3. **Sambuca Romana** - actually a drink, not a food, this anise-flavored liquor is served with one or two coffee beans in the bottom of the glass, called "mosche" (flies) by the Romans.

4. **Barba de frati** - literally monk's beard, this grass-like vegetable is unusual and good.

5. **Puntarelle** - a celery-like vegetable, served shaved into curls and dressed with oil, vinegar and anchovies.

6. **Casareccio** - local chewy bread.

7. **Fior di latte** - mozzarella made from cow's milk.

8. **Mozzarella di bufala** - mozzarella made from water buffalo milk.

9. **Ricotta** - fresh soft cheese, best eaten alone.

10. **Pecorino** - hard cheese made from sheep's milk; sometimes called Romano.

The Top 10 Best Places To Buy Gourmet and International Foods

1. Castroni
Several locations including Via Cola di Rienzo 196 and Piazza Medaglie d'Oro; features items from around the world, as well as Italian coffees, cakes, and ice creams.

2. Pannochi
Cakes and pastries, something to take to a Sunday dinner or to enjoy after a day of shopping.
Via Bergamo 56

3. Enoteca del Corso
Wines, cognacs, goodies, a great selection.
Corso V. Emanuele 293

4. L'Albero del Pane
Organic health foods (no produce), cosmetics, dietary supplements.
Via S. Maria del Pianto 19/20

5. Capone
Out-of-season fruits and vegetables, as well as olive oils and preserved foods.
Via G. Carini 39

6. Grand Gourmet
Wonderfully fresh and creative pasta.
Via C. Fracassini 15

7. Marcello
One of the best selections of fresh fish in Rome.
Via Tuscolana 1162

8. Antica Norcineria Viola
One of the last traditional pork butcheries.
Campo de' Fiori 43/c

9. La Cantina del Sud
Special foods from the south of Italy, including peppers, tomatoes, tuna, jams, cheeses and more from Calabria.
Borgo Pio 40

10. La Baronia
Fresh Italian cheeses.
Multiple locations including Via V. Lucchi 21 and Via Varrone 2/c

The Top 10 Romantic Places To Meet For A Drink

1. Le Grand Bar, St. Regis Grand Hotel
An elegant, old world ambience.
Via Vittorio Emanuele Orlando 3

2. Harry's Bar
Reminiscent of the 1950s La Dolce Vita era.
Via Veneto 150

3. The bar at Piazzale delle Muse
Nice view in an elegant neighborhood.
Off Viale Parioli

4. The Bar at the Cavalieri Hilton Hotel
A beautiful bar with a spectacular panoramic view of the city.
Via A. Cadlolo, 101

5. Zodiaco Bar on Monte Mario
Sit outside and enjoy the marvelous view.
Via Trionfale at Panoramica Rd.

6. Tre Scalini
A good place for a drink outside in Rome's most beautiful piazza.
Piazza Navona

7. The Excelsior Hotel Lobby Bar
Elegant, traditional, expensive.
Via Veneto at Via Ludovisi

8. The Eden Hotel
Just the name of this expensive hotel alone is evocative of romance.
Via Ludovisi, 49

9. Rosati ristorante
It's always romantic to sit drinking a Campari, overlooking the great piazza in the company of the literary lights and celebrities of Rome.
Piazza del Popolo

10. The Antico Caffé Greco
How romantic this is depends on how many beautiful presents he bought for her on the elegant Via Condotti.
Via Condotti, 86

The Top 10 Dancing And Discos

1. Gilda
Favorite of the Roman jetset, large dancefloor.
Via Mario de' Fiori 97

2. Soul II Soul
Via dei Fienaroli 30A

3. Argonauta
Moored paddle steamer, dancing Fridays and Saturdays.
Lungotevere degli Artigiani

4. Piper '90
Oldest and biggest Roman disco.
Via Tagliamento 9

5. El Charango
Salsa dancing.
Via di Sant'Onofrio 28

6. Yes Brazil
Bossa Nova.
Via S. Francesco a Ripa 103

7. Osiris
Rock.
Largo dei Librari 82A

8. The Open Gate
Latin disco, live music from Brazil.
Via San Nicolo di Tolentino 4

9. Qube
Rome's biggest underground disco.
Via di Portonaccio 212

10. Jackie O'
One of those places where you have to get past the doorman,
call first 0642885457.
Via Boncompagni

The Top 10 Things To Do At Night

For the truly romantic, there is nothing better to do at night than stroll the winding streets of ancient Rome. For those of a more exciting bent, here are the best pubs, bars, and music halls.

1. **Fantasie di Trastevere**
   Live floor show of Roman and Neapolitan music every evening except Sunday.
   Via di S. Dorotea 6, booking at Tel. 065894984.

2. **Gilda**
   Favorite nightclub of the Roman jetset.
   Via Mario de' Fiori 97

3. **Radio Londra Caffe**
   40's style establishment in a 1700s interior, live music daily except Tuesday.
   Via di Monte Testaccio.

4. **Rockodile Baja California**
   Classic rock music, sports TV on satellite.
   Via delle Tre Cannelle 8/9

5. **Il Salotto**
   Elegant pianobar
   Via G. Notaris 5

6. **The Abbey Theatre**
   Six rooms on two floors, Irish beer and whiskey.
   Via del Governo Vecchio 51/53

7. **The Black Duke**
   Disco pub on two floors, theme evenings every night.
   Via dei Cappellari 36

8. **Panico Biondo**
   Intimate piano bar with chanteuse Claudia Antro.
   Via di Panico 12

9. **Robin Hood**
   Labyrinthine pub with dozens of beers and forest atmosphere, open all night.
   Via Cavour 158

10. **Rock Castle**
    In the weapons room of an ancient palazzo, DJ nightly.
    Via Beatrice Cenci 8

The Top 10 Gay And Lesbian Activities And Places To Go

1. **www.publibyte.it/promo/consoli - connects to Gay House in Rome**
   Tel. 0693547567

2. **Babilona**
   Gay culture magazine, available at news kiosks.

3. **"Pianta Gay"**
   City map available at news kiosks.

4. **Edoardo II, music bar**
   Vicolo Margana 14

5. **Circolo Mario Mieli**
   Tel. 06 541 3985

6. **CLI (lesbian organization)**
   Tel. 066864201

7. **Informa Gay**
   Tel. Headquarters in Turin 011 4365000

8. **Alibi nightclub**
   Via di Monte Testaccio 44

9. **Hangar bar**
   Via in Selci 69

10. **Galaxia club**
    Women only Fridays and Saturday.
    Piazza Bulgarelli 41

The Top 10 Jazz Spots In Rome

Jazz became popular in Rome in the 1930s and interest grew after World War II, with the arrival of the Americans. In the 1950s the Roman New Orleans jazz band, which played Dixieland, thrilled audiences.

For information on current performances, check the Wanted in Rome and Where magazines, as well as Trova Roma, a weekly magazine published in Italian.

1. **Palladium**
   Piazza B. Romano 8

2. **Alpheus**
   Via del Commercio 36-38

3. **Vicolo 49**
   Vicolo dei Soldati 49

4. **Il Castello**
   Via Porta di Castello 44

5. **Caffe' les Folies**
   Via S. Francesco a Ripa

6. **Alexanderplatz**
   Via Ostia 9

7. **Mississippi Blues**
   Via del Mascherino 65

8. **Ciac Musica**
   Via Tripoli 60

9. **Saint Louis Music City**
   Via del Cardello 13

10. **Stardust**
    Vicolo de Renzi 4

The Top 10 Things To Do On Weekends

1. **Take a day trip outside** of Rome to see the countryside.

2. **Visit the Villa Borghese park** for a walk, a jog or to see the zoo.

3. **Visit the park at Villa Pamphilj** to fly a kite, walk the trails.

4. **Visit the park at Villa Ada** for pony rides, woodsy settings.

5. **Have brunch at the Cavalieri Hilton** overlooking the city.

6. **Visit one of the Roman Catholic or protestant churches.**

7. **Rent a bike** and ride out the Via Appia Antica in the morning and have lunch along the way

8. **Visit an exhibit at the Capitolini Museums.**

9. **Go to Europe's largest flea market** at Porta `Portese in Trastevere.

10. **Go to the English language movies.**

The Top 10 Expensive And Luxury Hotels In Rome

1. Rome Cavalieri Hilton

This five-star conference hotel offers the best view in Rome, as well as two excellent restaurants, a bank, travel agency, car rental and sporting facilities.
Via A. Cadlolo 101. Tel. 06 35091

2. Hassler

From its position atop the Spanish Steps, the Hassler offers five-star luxury in a reminder of an earlier, more extravagant time.
Piazza Trinita' dei Monti 6, Tel 06 678 2651

3. Eden

Five-star luxury in a late 19th century palazzo; many of the guest rooms have magnificent views of the city.
Via Ludovisi 49, Tel. 06 478121

4. Westin Excelsior Roma

Luxury and refinement are part and parcel of this beautiful five-star hotel steps away from the Villa Borghese gardens.
Via V. Veneto 125, Tel. 06 47081

5. St. Regis Grand (formerly Le Grand)

Re-opened as the St. Regis Grand after a $35 million restoration, this five-star aristocratic beauty offers sumptuous rooms and suites.
Via V.E. Orlando 3, Tel. 06 47091

6. L'Inghilterra

Liszt and Hemingway were among the early guests of the Hotel, built in 1850. This five-star facility is dead center of the haute couture shopping district.
Via Bocca di Leone 14, Tel. 06 672161

7. Parco dei Principi

Surrounded by greenery and opposite the Villa Borghese gardens, this is a five-star hotel in a tranquil setting.
Via G. Frescobaldi 5, Tel. 06 854521

8. Ponte Sisto

Within a restored 18th century building, this more recent addition to the five-star ranks is near the Campo de' Fiori; ask for the Belvedere room with its two panoramic terraces.
Via dei Pettinari 64, Tel. 06 686311

9. Lord Byron

Elegance and tranquility are imbued in this small five-star hotel with the famous Relais Le Jardin restaurant.
Via G. De Notaris 5, Tel. 06 3220404

10. Aldrovandi Palace

A refined hotel in a parklike setting, this five-star facility is inside a restored 19th century palazzo.

The Top 10 Moderately Priced Hotels In Rome

These hotels are not five-star, but they offer good value for the money.

1. Residenza Zanardelli
Charming, good location.
Via G. Zanardelli 7, near Piazza Navona, Tel.06 68211392

2. Hotel Navona
A less expensive sister to the Zanardelli.
Via dei Sediari 8, near Piazza Navona, Tel. 06 06 6864203

3. Hotel Miami
Good location near the train station.
Via Nazionale, 230

4. Hotel Domus Aventina
Quiet location on the Aventine Hill.
Via di Santa Prisca, 11B, Tel. 06 5746135

5. Palazzo al Velabro
Family hotel near the Bocca della Verita.
Via del Velabro 16, Tel. 06 6792758

6. Hotel Lancelot
Three-stars, near the Colosseum.
Via Capo D'Africa 47, Tel. 06 70450615

7. Hotel San Silvestro
Two-stars, near the Spanish Steps.
Via del Gambero 3, Tel. 06 6794169

8. Hotel Augustea
Three-stars, near the train station.
Via Via Nazionale 251, Tel. 06 4883589

9. Hotel Patria
Three-stars, convenient to tourist attractions.
Via Torino 36/37, Tel. 06 4880756

10. Hotel ISA
Three-stars, near the Vatican.
Via Cicerone 39, Piazza Cavour

The Top 10 Inexpensive Hotels And B&Bs In Rome

1. **Hotel Trastevere**
   Via Luciano Manara 24, Trastevere

2. **Fanny**
   Via A. Provana, 16, Piazza Ragusa

3. **Casa Giardino**
   Via Adamello, 6

4. **Marco**
   Lungotevere dei Mellini

5. **Maurizio B& B**
   Via L. A. Vassallo, 61

6. **Appennini**
   Via Appennini 32

7. **Green**
   Via dei Ciliegi, 27
   00040 Rocca Priora ,Castelli Romani

8. **Mailar**
   Lungotevere degli Artigiani, 10

9. **Bed and Breakfast Serra**
   Via Tito Omboni, 21

10. **Hotel Navona**
    Via dei Sediari 8

The Top 10 Romantic Hotels In Rome

1. **Albergo del Sole**
   Views of the Pantheon.
   Piazza della Rotonda, 63

2. **Hotel Carriage**
   Near the Spanish Steps with beautiful rooftop terrace; brass beds.
   Via delle Carrozze 36 , Tel. 06 6990124

3. **Hotel Gregoriana**
   Lovely rooms with breakfast served in the rooms.
   Via Gregoriana 18 , Tel. 06 6794269

4. **Hotel Hassler**
   Views and visiting royalty add cachet to the spectacular view.
   Piazza Trinità dei Monti 6 , Tel. 06 6782651

5. **Hotel d'Inghilterra**
   Passionate composer Franz Liszt stayed here; individually decorated bedrooms and a bar with the ambience of a London gentlemen's club.
   Via Bocca di Leone 14 , Tel. 06 672161

6. **Hotel Lord Byron**
   Charming and expensive, with pure linen sheets and bath towels, beautiful double rooms.
   Via G. de Notaris 5, Tel. 06 3220404

7. **Hotel Majestic**
   Eighteenth century style, lavish bathrooms, beautiful decor.
   Via V. Veneto 50 , Tel. 06 48641

8. **La Residenza**
   Like a private home, near the Via Veneto.
   Via Emilia, 22-24, Tel 06 4880789

9. **Hotel Raphael**
   A place for trysts on a cobbled street near the Piazza Navona.
   Largo Febo 2, Tel. 06 682831

10. **Hotel Margutta**
    Even the attic is romantic at this inexpensive hotel in the historic center.
    Via Laurina 34 , Tel. 06 3223674

The Top 10 Hotel Lobbies To Enjoy In Rome

Some have lobby bars, others are just beautiful settings to rest your feet or arrange a rendevous.

1. **Aldrovandi Palace**
   Via U. Aldrovandi 15

2. **Bernini Bristol**
   Piazza Barberini 23

3. **Crowne Plaza Roma Minerva**
   Piazza della Minerva 69

4. **D'Inghilterra**
   Via Bocca di Leone 14

5. **Eden Hotel**
   Via Ludovisi 49

6. **Excelsior Roma**
   Via Veneto 125

7. **Majestic Hotel**
   Via Veneto 50

8. **Massimo d'Azeglio**
   Via Cavour 18

9. **Parco dei Principi**
   Via G. Frescobaldi 5

10. **Ponte Sisto**
    Via dei Pettinari 64

The Top 10 Monasteries And Convents To Stay In

Many religious institutions in Rome take in paying guests. You do not have to be a practising Catholic to stay in one, but be sure to book well in advance. Some of them have curfews, so check first if you are a night owl. Places on this list take both men and women. Prices are in the same range as the cheapest hotels. To reserve, either write well in advance, fax to 39 0685301756, or email ilsogno@romeguide.it

1. Centro di Accoglienza Ma Maris Eugenia
Open all year.
Viale Romania, 32 (Parioli area)

2. Domus Aurelia
Closed August.
Via Aurelia, 218 (near St. Peter's)
00165 Roma

3. Domus Pacis Residence
Open all year.
Via di Torrerossa, 94 (Forte Aurelio area)
(piazza Carpegna) Tel. 6638791

4. Casa del Pellegrino del Santuario Madonna del Divino Amore
Open all year.
Loc. Castel di Leva - via Ardeatina, km 12
00134 Roma (Castel di Leva area)

5. Casa Domitilla
Open all year.
Via delle Sette Chiese, 280/282 (Garbatella area)
00147 Roma

6. Centro Accoglienza Villa Aurelia
Open all year.
Via Leone XIII, 459 (near St. Peter's)
00165 Roma

7. Istituto Suore Nostra Signora di Lourdes
Open all year.
Via Nostra Signora di Lourdes 2 (Quirinale area)
Roma

8. **Casa Beata Margherita**
   Via Fabio Massimo (Prati area)
   00192 Roma

9. **Casa Lopez Vicuna**
   Open all year.
   Via Palestro, 23 (near Termini)
   00185 Roma

10. **Casa Maria Immacolata**
    Via Ezio, 28 December 192(Prati area)

Emperor Augustus

The Top 10 Best Shopping Streets In Rome

1. **Via Condotti**
   The world famous street of designer fashions that runs between the Spanish Steps and Via Corso; great for window shopping and strolling

2. **Via Frattina**
   Parallel to Via Condotti, this street is full of beautiful shops

3. **Via Cola di Rienzo**
   Running from Piazza Risorgimento near the Vatican to the river, this street is home to dozens of clothing and shoe shops

4. **Via Bocca di Leone**
   Perpendicular to Via Condotti and home to Versace and friends

5. **Via Corso**
   At the end of Via Condotti, the Via Corso is a long street full of shops featuring knock offs of famous designs

6. **Via dei Coronari**
   Antique heaven, said by some (usually husbands) to be the street of coronaries because the prices bring on heart attacks

7. **Via del Babuino**
   One of the trident of streets that runs from the Piazza del Popolo toward the Spanish Steps, Via del Babuino is lined with sumptuous jewelry, clothing, art and fabric stores

8. **Via Borgognona**
   In the neighborhood of Via Condotti and stocked with designer fashions

9. **Via del Tritone**
   A street of bargain knock offs, much like Via Corso

10. **Via Propaganda/ Via Due Macelli**
    Twin streets that run from the Piazza di Spagna toward Via Tritone; Via Due Macelli is home to centuries old stationer, Pineider, as well as gift and leather goods shops, while Via Propaganda has Mandarina Duck, the luggage purveyor, and more leather goods.

The Top 10 Markets In Rome

Outdoor markets are a way of life in Rome, where inhabitants have shopped everyday for centuries. Some markets are a conglomeration of foodstuffs, linens, clothes and kitchen utensils; others specialize in one kind of merchandise or produce. The following is a list of the major outdoor markets and what they sell.

1. Campo de' Fiori
Centuries old market with meats, cheeses, produce, fish and flowers – visit it for its wonderful ambience.
Piazza Campo de' Fiori

2. Porta Portese
The largest flea market in Europe, 6:30 a.m. - 2 p.m. Sundays only, Porta Portese draws thousands of people each week and stretches for over a kilometer. Everything, from antiques to tools to kitchen supplies to food to pet supplies to linens to clothes, you-name-it, is for sale in Porta Portese on Sunday mornings. Prices negotiable.
Via Portuense &Via Ippolito Nievo

3. Mercato di Via Sannio
Second hand clothes, new clothes, shoes, bags, belts and more, this is the place to go if you're looking for a fashionable look for a low price. There is a great selection of leather jackets. Prices negotiable.
Via Sannio

4. Mercato delle Stampe
Old prints, books, magazines and, of course, stamps.
Largo della Fontanella di Borghese

5. Mercato dei Fiori
The Flower Market, open to the public only on Tuesdays. Absolutely gorgeous array of fresh flowers year round.
Via Trionfale

6. Mercato Andrea Doria
Fruit, vegetables, meat, clothes, shoes. One of dozens of similar street markets in Rome, this one is near St. Peter's.
Via Andrea Doria

7. Mercato di Testacio
Fruit, vegetables, fish, clothes, shoes. Similar to Andrea Doria.
Piazza Testaccio

8. Ponte Milvio

Fruit, vegetables, clothes, shoes and sometimes furniture; situated next to the ancient bridge, the Ponte Milvio. Antiques, along the River, first weekend of every month.
Piazza Ponte Milvio

9. Piazza dell' Unita

Fruit, vegetables, linens, purses right on one of Rome's most important shopping streets.
Via Cola di Rienzo

10. Piazza delle Coppelle

Fruit, food, flowers – a charming local market.
Near Pantheon

The Top 10 Streets To Find Bargains

Rome is known for its haute couture designers and world-class furnishings. But even the shopgirls are chic in the Eternal City because they know where to find less expensive copies of the latest styles and home designs. This list includes streets lined with shops featuring knockoffs of couture fashions, as well as a few outdoor markets.

1. Via Cappellari

Near the Campo d' Fiori outdoor market, this is a street lines with clothing and leather boutiques.

2. Via Corso

The street of knockoffs, both shoes and clothes.

3. Via Nazionale

More clothing boutiques.

4. Via del Tritone

Less expensive knockoffs.

5. Via Cavour

Less expensive knockoffs, old books and musical instruments.

6. Via Ottaviano

Clothing and shoes.

7. Via dei Giubbonari

Near Via Cappellari, with the same sort of stores.

8. Porta Portese market

Held in Trastevere every Sunday morning, Porta Portese is the largest flea market in Europe where shoppers can find almost anything.

9. Via Sannio market

Open every day near San Giovanni in Lateran church, this outdoor market sells clothes, shoes, used clothes and coats, leather goods, sports wear.

10. Via Andrea Doria market

Outdoor market near the Vatican, sells clothing, purses, shoes, foodstuffs, linens, kitchen items.

The Top 10 Best Streets For Art Galleries In Rome

Art and antiques dealers have congregated on these ancient streets for centuries. They are all in the historic center of Rome and many are close together.

1. **Via Guilia**
2. **Via Coronari**
3. **Via della Croce**
4. **Via Babuino**
5. **Via Margutta**
6. **Piazza di Spagna**
7. **Via Carrozze**
8. **Via dei Greci**
9. **Via Vittoria**
10. **Via della Frezza**

The Top 10 Women's Haute Couture In Rome

These are the designers seen in the fashion magazines, the clothes worn by the rich and famous. What's wonderful is that, not only do they have the latest designs, they will assist their customers in getting a return of the VAT tax. This makes a purchase up to 19% less expensive.

1. **Valentino**
   Piazza Mignanelli 22, Via Bocca di Leone 15

2. **Laura Biagiotti**
   Via Borgognona 43-44

3. **Mila Schon**
   Via Condotti 64-65

4. **Fendi**
   Via Borgognona 36A/39

5. **Genny**
   Piazza di Spagna 27

6. **Max Mara**
   Via Condotti 46

7. **Gianfranco Ferre**
   Via Borgognona 42C

8. **Giorgio Armani**
   Via Condotti 77

9. **Gucci**
   Via Condotti 4

10. **Versace**
    Via Bocca di Leone 26

The Top 10 Places To Buy Men's Clothes

Italian men are known for their clothes; the care they take in dressing and looking good is a great part of their charm. The clothiers below offer the highest quality menswear and most will provide assistance to customers wishing to file for the return of the VAT tax. Some, like Versace, Gucci and Valentino, offer high fashion looks, while the others sell more traditional clothing.

1. **Brioni**
   Via Barberini 79

2. **Battistoni**
   Via Condotti 57 and 61A

3. **Galtrucco**
   Piazza S. Claudio 167

4. **Gucci**
   Via Condotti 8

5. **Versace Uomo**
   Via Borgognona 29

6. **Valentino Uomo**
   Via Condotti 13

7. **Osvaldo Testa**
   Via Borgognona 13,Via Frattina 104

8. **Cucci**
   Via Condotti 67

9. **Enzo Ceci**
   Via della Vite 52

10. **Carlo Palazzi**
    Via Borgognona 7E

The Top 10 Shoe Stores In Rome

Italian shoes are known the world over for their style, quality, and fit. This is a list of the finest brands. Many will assist customers in filing for the return of the VAT tax. The shoe stores along Via Corso, as well as shoe vendors in the outdoor markets, offer the styles of the season at lower prices.

1. **Ferragamo**
   The best selection of Ferragamos outside of Florence, men and women.
   Via Condotti 73-74

2. **Bruno Magli**
   High fashion looks, as well as traditional styles for men and women.
   Via del Gambero 1, Via Veneto 70A

3. **Fratelli Rossetti**
   Elegant, fashionable selection, men and women.
   Via Borgognona 5A

4. **Campanile**
   Good selection, good end-of-season sales.
   Via Condotti 58

5. **Pollini**
   A favorite of Romans, more moderately priced.
   Via Frattina 22-24

6. **Mario Valentino**
   Leather clothing, bags and shoes.
   Via Frattina 84

7. **Raphael Salato**
   Fashion forward styles, intricate designs, expensive.
   Via Veneto 149

8. **Albanese**
   Shoes made to measure, expensive.
   Via Carlo Dossi 71

9. **De Bach**
   Good selection of shoes for women.
   Via Babuino 123

10. **Faust Santini**
    Less expensive styles for younger people.

The Top 10 Department Stores And Malls In Rome

1. **Coin Department Store**
   Via Cola di Rienzo 173
   Piazzale Appio 7

2. **Upim Department Stores**
   Various locations including Via del Tritone 172

3. **La Rinascente Department Store**
   Via del Corso 189

4. **Cinecitta' Due Centro Commerciale mall**
   Via Tuscolana

5. **Tucano**
   Various Locations

6. **I Granai Mall**
   Via Laurentina

7. **Prenatal Maternity Clothing**
   Various locations around Rome

8. **Metro Wholesale Warehouses**

9. **Coop**
   Walmart kind of store - various locations in suburbs
   Via Laurentina

10. **Pym and GS supermarket chains**
    Various locations around the city
    Via U. Aldrovandi 15, Tel. 06 3223993

The Top 10 Jewelry Stores In Rome

Italians are known for their artistry in working with gold. Though there are dozens of small jewelers to discover, this list includes the most famous. Most of them provide assistance for customers who wish to have the VAT tax refunded at the airport.

1. **Bulgari**
   Via Condotti 10

2. **Buccellati**
   Via Condotti 31

3. **Cartier**
   Via Condotti 82/83

4. **Ansuini**
   Via del Babuino 150D

5. **Massoni**
   Largo Carlo Goldoni 48

6. **Moroni Gioielli**
   Via Belsiana 32A

7. **Petocchi**
   Piazza di Spagna 23

8. **Peroso**
   Via Sistina 29

9. **Boncompagni Sterni**
   Via del Babuino 115

10. **Ouroboros**
    Via di Sant'Eustachio 14

The Top 10 Tableware Shops In Rome

1. **Spazio Sette**
   Beautiful multi-level store filled with contemporary furniture and accessories.
   Via dei Barbieri 7

2. **Tupini**
   Quality china, glass and silverware.
   Piazza S. Lorenzo in Lucina

3. **Richard Ginori**
   Famous name in ceramics
   Via Cola di Rienzo 223
   Via del Tritone 177

4. **Venini**
   Spectacular glassware.
   Via del Babuino 130

5. **Stilvetro**
   Less expensive ceramics and glass.
   Via Frattina 56

6. **C.u.c.i.n.a.**
   Basement store filled with contemporary kitchenware.
   Via del Babuino 118A

7. **Single**
   Stainless steel designs like Alessi and wooden breadboards.
   Via Francesco Crispi 45-47

8. **Modigliani**
   The ideal place to buy a wedding gift.
   Via Condotti 24

9. **Frette home couture**
   Fine quality linens and items for the home.
   Piazza di Spagna 11

10. **Arteque**
    Beautiful shop with traditional items.
    Via Giulia 13

The Top 10 Size And Measurement Charts

Everything in Italy is measured on the Metric System. If you are unsure of the size you want, go up a size rather than down because many things run smaller than their American or British size equivalent. House wine can be ordered in a restaurant by the liter, half liter or quarter liter or "quartino."

1. **1 liter =** 33.5 fluid ounces

2. **.4732 liter =** 1 pint

3. **¼ liter =** 8.5 fluid ounces

4. **Women's clothes**
   US Size 2 (Ital. 36) Size 4 (It. 38) Size 6 (40) Size 8 (42) Size 10 (44) Size 12 (46) Size 14 (48) Size 16 (50) Size 18 (52)

5. **Men's shirts**
   US Size 15 (Ital. 38) Size 15.5 (39) Size 16 (40) Size 16.5 (41) Size 17 (42) Size 17.5 (43)

6. **Men's Trousers**
   US Size 30 (Ital. 46) Size 32 (48) Size 34 (50) Size 36 (52) Size 38 (54) Size 40 (56)

7. **Men's Suits/Jackets**
   US Size 38 (Ital. 48) Size 40 (50) Size 42 (52) Size 44 (54) Size 46 (56) Size 48 (58)

8. **Children's Clothes**
   US Size 4 (Ital. 50) Size 6 (60) Size 8 (70) Size 10 (80) Size 12 (90)

9. **Women's Shoes**
   US Size 5.5 (Ital. 35) Size 6.5 (36) Size 7 (37) Size 7.5 (38) Size 8 (38.5) Size 9 (39-40) Size 10 (41)

10. **Men's Shoes**
    US Size 7.5 (Ital. 41) Size 8 (41.5) Size 9 (42.5) Size 9.5 (43) Size 10 (43.5) Size11 (44 - 44.5) Size 12 (44.5)

The Top 10 Beauty Parlors In Rome

Roman women tend to wear their hair much longer than Americans, even at later stages of life. Still, their hair is beautiful, well taken care of, and perfectly colored. These salons are only suggestions. Don't do anything drastic without seeing the results worked on other customers. You're safe with a manicure or pedicure as a first look at the salon. If you like it, make another appointment for cut or color.

1. **Arte e Bellezza**
   Piazza di Spagna 35

2. **Beauty Planet**
   Grand Hotel Palace, Via Veneto 66-70

3. **Elleffe**
   Via di San Calisto 6

4. **F&M Aveda-Roma Concept Day Spa**
   Rampa Mignanelli 9

5. **Mauro Lulli**
   Piazza Trinita dei Monti 6

6. **I Sargassi**
   Via Frattina 48

7. **Sergio Valente**
   Via Condotti 11

8. **Mino Moretti**
   Via dei Clementino 101

9. **Alfredo Trotta**
   Via de Regina Margherita 64

10. **Fabrizio**
    Via Nomentana 251

The Top 10 Antiques Shops In Rome

Whole streets, such as Via del Babuino, Via dei Coronari, Via Giulia and Via Margutta are filled with antique shops. These are some of the best.

1. **W Apolloni**
   Prestigious, attracts professional collectors, 17th century items.
   Via del Babuino 132

2. **Amedeo di Castro**
   Fourth-generation dealer, bas-relief sculptures, 18th-19th century items.
   Via del Babuino 77

3. **Granmercato Antiquario Babuino**
   Silver, porcelain, small collectors pieces from the 17th century.
   Via del Babuino 150

4. **La Chimera**
   Neo-classical furniture and paintings.
   Via Giulia 122

5. **Antiquariato Valligiano**
   The only place to find 19th century Italian country furniture.
   Via Giulia 193

6. **Art Deco Gallery**
   Furniture and sculpture.
   Via dei Coronari 14

7. **Retrospettiva**
   Furniture, Murano glass and Faenza pottery from 1900-50.
   Via del Boschetto 77A

8. **Alberto di Castro Antichita' e Grafica Antica**
   Fine antiques and graphics.
   Via del Babuino 71

9. **La Soffitta della Nonna**
   Grandma's attic – fun to look around.
   Via della Scrofa 48

10. **Fratelli Agostinelli**
    For serious collectors.
    Via D. Bartolemeo 42

The Top 10 Bookstores In Rome/ English And Italian

1. Rizzoli
One of the top publishers in Italy, more traditional in scope.
Largo Chigi 15; Via Tomacelli 156

2. Fetrinelli
A top publisher, more radical in scope; offers books in many languages.
Via V.E. Orlando 78, Via del Babuino 39-41

3. Franco Maria Ricci
Expensive art books.
Via Borgognona 4D

4. Libreria Godel
Books on Rome, second-hand art books.
Via Poli 45

5. Libreria San Silvestro, aka Remainders
Wonderful selection of remainders, including art books, in Italian.
Piazza San Silvestro 27

6. The Vatican bookstore
Books on art and religion.
St. Peter's Square

7. The Lion Bookshop
British-owned, good selection of books in English.
Via dei Greci 36

8. The Corner Bookshop
One of Trastevere's English bookshop, good selection and ambience.
Via del Moro 48

9. The Open Door Bookshop
In Trastevere, good selection.
Via della Lungaretta 25

10. Libreria 4 Fontane
International selection in many languages.
Via Quattro Fontane 20A

The Top 10 Types Of Stores In Rome

Italy is a country where most goods are purchased in a store specializing in one type of merchandise. To find what you're looking for, use this list.

1. **Forno**
   Bread store

2. **Pasticceria**
   Bakery

3. **Frutteria**
   Fruit and vegetables

4. **Ferramenta**
   Hardware

5. **Enoteca**
   Wine

6. **Alimentari**
   General grocery store

7. **Tabacchi (signified with black T on white background)**
   Tobacco, stamps, bus tickets

8. **Bancomat**
   ATM machine

9. **Casalinghi**
   Housewares

10. **Parrucchiera**
    Hairdresser

10 More Types Of Stores In Rome

1. **Merceria**
   Sewing supplies, handerchiefs, underwear

2. **Edicola**
   Newspaper kiosk

3. **Grandi magazzini**
   Department stores

4. **Macelleria**
   Butcher shop

5. **Panetteria**
   Bread shop, bakery

6. **Tintorla**
   Dry cleaner

7. **Lavanderia**
   Laundromat

8. **Paninoteca**
   Sandwich shop

9. **Cartoleria**
   Stationery shop

10. **Libreria**
    Bookstore

The Top 10 English Bookstores And Libraries

1. **British Council Library**
   Via delle Quattro Fontane, 20,
   Tel 06478141

2. **Santa Susanna Lending Library**
   Via XX Settembre 15
   Tel 064827510

3. **The Anglo American Bookshop**
   Via della Vite 102
   Tel 066795222

4. **The Corner Bookshop**
   Via del Moro 48
   Tel 065836942

5. **The Economy Book and Video Center**
   Via Torino 136
   Tel 064746877

6. **The Open Door Bookshop**
   Via della Lungaretta 25
   Tel 065896478

7. **Keats-Shelley Memorial**
   Piazza di Spagna 26
   Tel 066784235

8. **English Bookshop**
   Via Ripetta 248
   Tel 063203301

9. **Feltrinelli (English Section)**
   Largo di Torre Argentina 5
   Tel 0668808160

10. **Rizzoli (English Section)**
    Largo Chigi 15,
    Tel 066796641.

Phrases

The Top 10 Italian Phrases For Travelers

In Italian you must pronounce every letter; there are no silent letters. When you see the letter "e" at the end of the word, it should be pronounced "a." Otherwise, do your best or take an Italian course.

1. **I have nothing to declare.**
   Non ho nulla da dichiarare.

2. **Where is the bathroom?**
   Dove' la toilette?

3. **Please, slow down**
   Rallenti, per favore.

4. **I would like to go to the train station**
   Vorrei andare all astazione.

5. **Local trains (stopping at every station)**
   Diretto or accelerato.

6. **Nonstop trains**
   Espresso and rapido.

7. **Call me a taxi**
   Mi chiami un taxi.

8. **Here's something for your trouble**
   Questo per il disturbo.

9. **Stop thief!**
   Al ladro!

10. **Could I have an English speaking operator?**
    Puo' passarmi un centralinista che parla inglese?

10 More Italian Phrases For Travelers

1. **Make that a collect call.**
   A spese ricevente, per favore.

2. **How much does it cost?**
   Quanto verra' a costare? or, Quanto costa?

3. **Fill it up, please**
   Il pieno, per favore.

4. **I am truly sorry**
   Mi dispiace davvero.

5. **Do you have it in another color?**
   Ne ha di un altro colore?

6. **How long will they be on strike?**
   Quanto tempo staranno in sciopero?

7. **Thank you so much**
   Grazie mille or grazie tante.

8. **I'll call the police**
   Chiamo la polizia.

9. **Help!**
   Aiuto!

10. **Leave me alone**
    Mi lasci in pace

Trinita dei Monti

The Top 10 Phrases For Meeting People

1. **Piacere (short for piacere di conoscerla)**
   Pleased to meet you.

2. **Come sta?**
   How are you? How do you do?

3. **Buon giorno**
   good morning or good day.

4. **Sono molto lieto di fare la sua conoscenza**
   I am very pleased to meet you.

5. **Ecco il mio biglietto da vista**
   Here is my card.

6. **Posso chiederle chi e'?**
   May I ask who you are?

7. **Lei parla inglese?**
   Do you speak English?

8. **Non parlo bene italiano**
   I don't speak Italian well.

9. **Le chiedo scusa**
   I beg your pardon?

10. **Si segga**
    Please be seated.

The Top 10 Phrases To Use When Traveling Together In Rome

1. We would like...
Voremmo…

2. The lady would like...
La signora vorrebbe…

3. A room with a double bed
Una camera con letto matrimoniale.
(Usually it will be queen or king sized.)

4. I pray
Prego.
(Used to indicate someone else should go first.)

5. Permission to enter someone else's house or room
Permesso

6. Two tickets
Due biglietti

7. Where can we go to dance?
Dove possiamo andare a ballare?

8. Where shall we meet?
Dove possiamo incontrarci?

9. I would like to reserve a table for two.
Vorrei riservare una tavola per due.

10. Two rooms
Due camere

The Top 10 Direction Phrases To Use In Rome

1. **Where is/Where are... ?**
   Dove/ Dove sono…?

2. **How do I get to... ?**
   Come faccio per arrivare a…?

3. **It is on the left/on the right.**
   E' a sinistra/a destra.

4. **Can you show me on the map where I am?**
   Puo' indicarmi sulla cartina dove me trovo?

5. **You are on the wrong street.**
   E' sulla strada sbagliata.

6. **Go straight ahead.**
   Continui diritto

7. **How long does it take to get to ... ?**
   Quanto tempo ci vuole per andare a …?

8. **Bus stop**
   La fermata dell'autobus

9. **Railway station**
   La stazione

10. **Tourist information**
    L'ufficio turistico

Pieta

The Top 10 Phrases To Use Regarding Hotels In Rome

1. **I made a reservation.**
   Ho fatto una prenotazione.

2. **I'd like a room with a bath/shower.**
   Vorrei una camera con bagno/ con doccia.

3. **What is the price per night?**
   Qual e' il prezzo per una notte?

4. **May I see the room?**
   Posso vedere la camera?

5. **What is the number of my room?**
   Qual'e il numero della mia camera?

6. **Is the room with air conditioning?**
   E' la camera con condizionamento dell'aria?

7. **Do you have any vacant rooms?**
   Avete camere libere?

8. **May I have the key?**
   Posso avere la chiave?

9. **Porter**
   Il facchino (fac-keyno)

10. **A double room/room with two beds/ single room**
    Una camera doppia/con due letti/singola

The Top 10 Numbers To Use In Rome

1. uno (oo-no)
2. due (do-A)
3. tre (tray)
4. quattro (quat-trO)
5. cinque (chin-quay)
6. sei (say)
7. sette (she-tay)
8. otto (O-toe)
9. nove (no-vey)
10. dieci (dee-eh-chay)

The Top 10 Time Terms To Use In Rome

1. **Mattina**
   Morning

2. **Mezzogiorno**
   Noon

3. **Pomeriggio**
   Afternoon

4. **Sera**
   Evening

5. **Notte**
   Night

6. **Mezzonotte**
   Midnight

7. **Ora**
   Hour

8. **Minuto**
   Minute

9. **Giorno**
   Day

10. **Secondo**
    Second

Top Ten Calendar Terms In Rome

1. **Domenica**
   Sunday

2. **Lunedi**
   Monday

3. **Martedi**
   Tuesday

4. **Mercoledi**
   Wednesday

5. **Giovedi**
   Thursday

6. **Venerdi**
   Friday

7. **Sabato**
   Saturday

8. **Settimana**
   Week

9. **Mese**
   Month

10. **Anno**
    Year

10 Months Plus Two In Rome

1. **Gennaio**
   January

2. **Febbraio**
   February

3. **Marzo**
   March

4. **Aprile**
   April

5. **Maggio**
   May

6. **Giugno**
   June

7. **Iuglio**
   July

8. **Agosto**
   August

9. **Settembre**
   September

10. **Ottobre**
    October

11. **Novembre**
    November

12. **Dicembre**
    December

The Top 10 Words For Color In Rome

1. **Nero**
   Black

2. **Bianco**
   White

3. **Rosso**
   Red

4. **Giallo**
   Yellow

5. **Verde**
   Green

6. **Blu**
   Blue

7. **Marrone**
   Brown

8. **Rosa**
   Pink

9. **Viola**
   Purple

10. **Grigio**
    Gray

The Top 10 Gracious Phrases

1. **Grazie**
   Thank you

2. **Prego**
   Used to let someone else go first or as your welcome

3. **Per favore**
   Please

4. **Arrivederci**
   Good bye

5. **Buon giorno**
   Good morning or good day

6. **Buona sera**
   Good afternoon

7. **Buona notte**
   Good night

8. **Mi scusi**
   Excuse me

9. **Entri, prego**
   Please, come in

10. **Torni a visitarci**
    Please come again

The Top 10 Phrases Of Celebration

1. **Auguri**
   Best wishes

2. **Buon natale**
   Merry Christmas

3. **Buon anno**
   Happy New Year

4. **Buon compleanno**
   Happy Birthday

5. **Buona Pasqua**
   Happy Easter

6. **Buona fortuna**
   Good luck

7. **Felicitazioni / congratulazioni**
   Congratulations

8. **Che dio ti benedica**
   God bless you (for this)!

9. **Che bella sorpresa!**
   What a surprise!

10. **Meraviglioso!/Stupendo!/Fantastico!**
    Marvelous/stupendous/fantastic

The Top 10 Words And Phrases About Seafood In Rome

Roman ristoranti are full of seafood dishes. The following list will help you determine what you want, and what you don't want, to order. Most fish will arrive at the table whole. The waiter will be happy to dehead and debone a fish for a customer. If you don't want to look a fish in the eye, order a filetto.

1. **Spigola**
Bass

2. **Orata**
Bream

3. **Vongole**
Clams, usually come in the shell

4. **Baccala**
Dried cod, a specialty in the Jewish Ghetto

5. **Merluzzo**
Fresh cod

6. **Granchio**
Crab

7. **Aragosta**
Lobster

8. **Cozze**
Mussels, often served in the shells in a succulent broth

9. **Passera**
Flounder

10. **Scampi**
Prawns, usually served in the shell

10 More Words About Seafood

1. **Salmone**
   Salmon

2. **Gamberetti**
   Shrimp, usually served in the shell

3. **Sogliola**
   Sole

4. **Pesce spada**
   Swordfish, usually served as a filet

5. **Trota**
   Trout

6. **Tonno**
   Tuna

7. **Sgombro or Maccarello**
   Mackerel

8. **Anguilla**
   Eel

9. **Alici or Acciughe**
   Anchovies

10. **Persico**
    Perch

The Top 10 Plus Five Italian Words For Fruit

Fresh fruit is often served as a dessert in a restaurant. It is also a major ingredient in gelati. In the summer, it's wonderful to ask for a slice of watermelon or a bowl of fresh strawberries with a squeeze of lemon after a large meal.

1. **Mele**
   Apples

2. **Albicocche (albi coki)**
   Apricots

3. **More (moray)**
   Blackberries

4. **Ciliege (chilli age y)**
   Cherries

5. **Fichi (feeky)**
   Figs

6. **Pompelmo**
   Grapefruit

7. **Uva (oova)**
   Grapes

8. **Pesche (pesky)**
   Peaches

9. **Pere (per ay)**
   Pears

10. **Fragole (frag ole')**
    Strawberries

11. **Cocomero**
    Watermelon

12. **Arance (aran chee ay)**
    Oranges

13. **Meloni**
    Melons, such as cantelope

14. **Limoni**
    Lemons

15. **Ananas**
    Pineapple

The Top 10 Words For Vegetables In Rome

Italians are known for their fresh vegetables, many of which are eaten at room temperature with olive oil, salt and a squeeze of lemon. Others, such as broccoli, can be sauteed in olive oil and garlic and served warm. Still others are delicious grilled with a drizzle of olive oil on top.

1. **Asparagi**
   Asparagus

2. **Carciofi (car cho fee)**
   Artichokes

3. **Fagioli (fah joe lee)**
   Beans

4. **Carote (care o' tay)**
   Carrots

5. **Cavolfiore**
   Cauliflower

6. **Melanzana**
   Eggplant

7. **Funghi (foon ghee)**
   Mushrooms

8. **Cipolle (chee pole ee)**
   Onions

9. **Patate**
   Potatoes

10. **Pomodori**
    Tomatoes

The Top 10 Words For Meat In Rome

Romans eat veal cooked in a variety of ways. They also love pork and beef. Turkey is showing up more often in supermarkets and restaurants, and ostrich meat (struzzi) is occasionally an option. This list is primarily composed of meats to be ordered in a restaurant. A warning: sometimes Italian restaurants offer a menu translated into English which isn't exactly accurate.

1. **Manzo, bistecca**
   Beef

2. **Vitello**
   Veal

3. **Agnello**
   Lamb

4. **Prosciutto cotto**
   Baked ham

5. **Prosciutto crudo**
   Cured ham

6. **Bresaola**
   Dried beef, often served in a kind of salad with arugula and parmesan

7. **Maiale**
   Pork

8. **Salsiccia**
   Sausage

9. **Pollo**
   Chicken

10. **Faraona**
    Guinea hen

The Top 10 Words To Use When Buying Leather Goods

Italians are known for their leather goods. This list will be helpful when shopping for leather items. Many outdoor stalls sell leather goods - be aware that these, while genuine leather, will not be the same quality as those sold in fine stores.

1. **Cintura**
   Belt

2. **Cartella**
   Briefcase

3. **Camoscio or pelle scamosciata**
   Suede

4. **Borsa**
   Handbag

5. **Valigia**
   Suitcase

6. **Capretto**
   Kid

7. **Portafoglio**
   Wallet

8. **Guanti**
   Gloves

9. **Vitello**
   Calfskin

10. **Cinghiale**
    Pigskin

The Top 10 Words To Use When Buying Cosmetics In Rome

Enticing Roman profumerie (perfume and cosmetics shops) are located on almost every street. Their creatively decorated windows advertise everything from make up to hair ornaments and costume jewelry. One of the most interesting is Ai Monasteri, Piazza delle Cinque Lune 76, near the Piazza Navona, where everything is made by monks from monasteries around Italy.

1. **Fondotinta**
   Blush

2. **Ombretto**
   Eyeshadow

3. **Eyeliner/mascara**
   Eyeliner/mascara

4. **Pettine**
   Comb

5. **Sottocipria**
   Foundation

6. **Spazzola**
   Hairbrush

7. **Rossetto**
   Lipstick

8. **Smalto**
   Nail polish

9. **Solvente or Acetone**
   Nail polish remover

10. **Profumo**
    Perfume

The Top 10 Words To Use When Buying Men's Clothes

Italian clothes for men are among the most beautiful in the world, but only if they fit properly. The following list will help you in buying men's clothing and having it tailored.

1. **Sarto**
   Tailor

2. **Cintura**
   Belt

3. **Giacca**
   Jacket

4. **Revers**
   Lapels

5. **Soprabito**
   Overcoat

6. **Tasche**
   Pockets

7. **Abito**
   Suit

8. **Pantaloni**
   Trousers

9. **Risvolti dei pantaloni**
   Cuffs

10. **Vita**
    Waistline

The Top 10 Words To Know When Buying Shoes In Rome

There is nothing like a beautiful pair of Italian shoes and in Rome the possibilities are endless. While shops like Bruno Magli and Ferragamo sell top-of-the-line shoes, the shops along the Via Corso and Via Cola di Rienzo offer opportunities to purchase well-made Italian shoes with brand names you've never heard. Chances are that many of these brands are sold in the US under private store labels at prices much higher. Don't forget that if you do buy from the high profile stores, it's possible to get almost twenty percent of the purchase price back at the airport if the cost is over 300,000 lire.

1. **Calzature**
   Shoes, shoe shop

2. **Stivali**
   Boots

3. **Comodo**
   Comfortable

4. **Tacchi**
   Heels

5. **Lacci or Stringhe**
   Laces

6. **Sandali**
   Sandals

7. **Scarpe**
   Shoes

8. **Misura**
   Size

9. **Pantofole**
   Slippers

10. **Suole**
    Soles

The Top 10 Medical Words And Phrases In Rome

In Rome, the pharmacies (farmacia) are marked with a green cross. There is a rotation of shops that stay open in the evening - these are listed in the daily newspaper. The pharmacists, many of them women, are very well trained and helpful. If you are able to show them an empty package, they will sometimes be able to replenish your medicines without a prescription or provide a good substitute. The following is a list of words that may be helpful to you in a pharmacy.

1. **Antisettico**
   Antiseptic

2. **Aspirina**
   Aspirin (sometimes comes with vitamin C in tablets that fizz in water)

3. **Benda or Cerotto**
   Bandage

4. **Cotone**
   Cotton wool

5. **Siringa ipodermica**
   Syringe

6. **Medicina**
   Medicine

7. **Pillole**
   Pills

8. **Prescrizione medica or ricetta**
   Prescription

9. **Assorbenti igienici**
   Sanitary napkins

10. **Tampone**
    Tampon

The Top 10 Words Used In An Office In Rome

1. **L'agenda**
   Appointment book

2. **La scrivania**
   Desk

3. **La diplomatica**
   Briefcase

4. **Il cestino**
   Wastebasket

5. **La fotocopiatrice**
   Photocopier

6. **La matita**
   Pencil

7. **La scheda/l'archivio**
   File

8. **Il pennarello**
   Magic marker

9. **Il calcolatore**
   Calculator

10. **L'evidenziatore**
    Highlighter

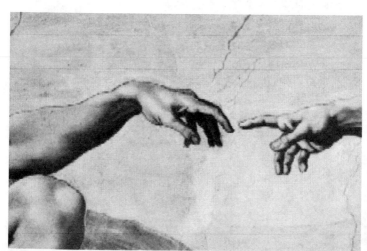

Ceiling of the Sistine Chapel

The Top 10 Curses Used in Rome

Even elegant Roman women are heard to use the most incredible curses. For a visitor to Italy, knowing an appropriate curse can be useful, but it is wise to toss a curse only from a moving vehicle so as to avoid retribution.

1. **Rude**
   Maleducato

2. **Turd/Female Turd**
   Stronzo/stronza

3. **Cretin**
   Cretino

4. **Go screw yourself!**
   Vaffanculo

5. **What a jerk!**
   Pezzo di stupido

6. **Are you crazy?**
   Ma sei matto?

7. **Sissy!**
   Frocio!

8. **You're disgusting!**
   Fa schifo!

9. **A curse on your dead relatives!**
   Ma li mortacci tua!

10. **Used for negative astonishment, especially for high prices or exaggeration**
    E'la Madonna!

The Top 10 Movies Set In Rome

1. **Rome Adventure (1962:US)**
   With Troy Donahue, Suzanne Pleschette, Angie Dickinson and Rossano Brazzi.

2. **Roman Holiday (1953:US)**
   With Audrey Hepburn and Gregory Peck. Hepburn won an Oscar for this one.

3. **The Bicycle Thief/Ladri di Biciclette (1949:Italy)**
   Was Vittorio DeSica's Academy Award winning classic.

4. **Three Coins in the Fountain (1954:US)**
   With Dorothy McGuire, Jean Peters, Rossano Brazzi, Louis Jourdan, and Clifton Webb.

5. **La Dolce Vita (1960:Italy)**
   Anita Ekberg and Marcello Mastroianni directed by Federico Fellini.

6. **The Roman Spring of Mrs. Stone (1961:Great Britian)**
   Based on a novella by Tennessee Williams, it stars Vivian Leigh and Warren Beatty (as her Italian gigolo).

7. **Open City/Roma, Citta Aperta (1946:Italy)**
   Roberto Rossellini directs Anna Magnani and Aldo Fabrizi.

8. **Gladiator (2000:USA)**
   A modern classic with Russell Crowe.

9. **Roma (1972: Italy-France)**
   No plot here, just Fellini's lifelong relationship with Rome.

10. **Spartacus, Ben Hur, Cleopatra, Quo Vadis**
    Each one is about life in ancient Rome.

The Top 10 Sayings About Rome

1. **"All roads lead to Rome."**
   La Fontaine, Fables, XII

2. **"Rome was not built in a day."**
   Cervantes, *Don Quixote*

3. **"When they are in Rome, they do there as they see done."**
   (When in Rome, do as the Romans do)
   Burton, *Anatomy of Melancholy, III*

4. **"Not that I loved Caesar less, but I loved Rome more."**
   Shakespeare, *Julius Caesar,* III, 2

5. **"To The Senate and People of Rome (S.P.Q.R.)."**
   Motto of Rome.

6. **"I found Rome brick and left it marble."**
   Caesar Augustus.

7. **"Butchered to make a Roman holiday."**
   Byron, *Childe Harold,* IV

8. **"Everyone soon or late comes round by Rome."**
   Robert Browning

9. **"Friends, Romans and countrymen, lend me your ears: I come to bury Caesar, not to praise him."**
   Shakespeare, *Julius Caesar,* Act III

10. **"To all that be in Rome, beloved of God, called to be saints: Grace to you and peace from God our Father, and the Lord Jesus Christ."**
    The Epistle of Paul the Apostle to the Romans

The Top 10 Books About Rome

1. **The Marble Faun** by Nathaniel Hawthorne

2. **Quo Vadis** by W. S. Kuniczak (Translator), Henryk K. Sienkiewicz

3. **The Rise and Fall of the Roman Empire** by Montesquieux

4. **History of Rome** by Mommsen

5. **History of Rome** by Thomas Carlyle

6. **As Romans Do** by Alan Epstein

7. **City Secrets: Rome** edited by Robert Kahn

8. **The Aeneid** by Virgil

9. **The Ancient Roman City** by John Stambaugh

10. **The Ancient Romans** by Chester Starr

The Top 10 Songs In Rome

1. **Three Coins in the Fountain** by Jules Styne and Sammy Cahn from the movie of the same name

2. **Arriverderci Roma** by Renato Rascel

3. **Que Sera, Sera** by Jay Livingston and Ray Evans from the movie The Man Who Knew Too much

4. **Theme from La Dolce Vita** directed by Federico Fellini

5. **The Fountains of Rome** by Respighi

6. **The Pines of Rome** by Respighi

7. **Roman Carnival** by Donizetti

8. **The Fountains of the Villa d'Este** by Liszt

9. **Suona, Suona Mia Chitarra** sung by Connie Francis

10. **Italian Impressions** by Charpentier

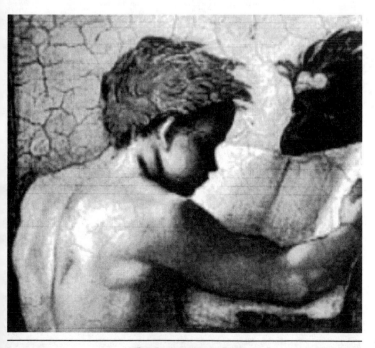

The Top 10 Plays And Operas About Rome

1. **Tosca** by Puccini (opera)

2. **Julius Caesar** by Shakespeare

3. **Antony and Cleopatra** by Shakespeare

4. **Antony and Cleopatra** by Samuel Barber (opera)

5. **Nerone** by Arrigo Boito (opera)

6. **The Rape of Lucretia** by Benjamin Britten

7. **Lucrezia Borgia** by Donizetti (opera)

8. **Agrippina** by Handel (opera)

9. **La Clemenza di Tito** by Mozart (opera)

10. **L'incoronazione di Poppea** by Monteverdi (opera)

The Top 10 Celebrities Connected With Rome

1. **Federico Fellini,** film director

2. **Gina Lollobrigida,** actress

3. **Sophia Loren,** actress

4. **Anna Magnani,** actress

5. **Audrey Hepburn,** actress

6. **Isabella Rossellini,** actress

7. **Ingrid Bergman,** actress

8. **Anthony Quinn,** actor

9. **Elizabeth Taylor,** actress

10. **Marcello Mastroianni,** actor

The Top 10 Designers Connected With Rome

1. **Rocco Barrocco**
2. **Brioni**
3. **Guy Matti0oli**
3. **Lorenza Riva**
5. **Valentino**
6. **Battistoni**
7. **Kenzo**
8. **Capucci**
9. **Bulgari**
10. **Laura Biagiotti**

The Top 10 Writers Who Wrote In Or About Rome

1. Lord Byron
2. John Keats
3. Percy B. Shelley
4. Mary Shelley
5. John Milton
6. Henry James
7. Alberto Moravia
8. Robert Browning
9. Montaigne
10. VIrgil

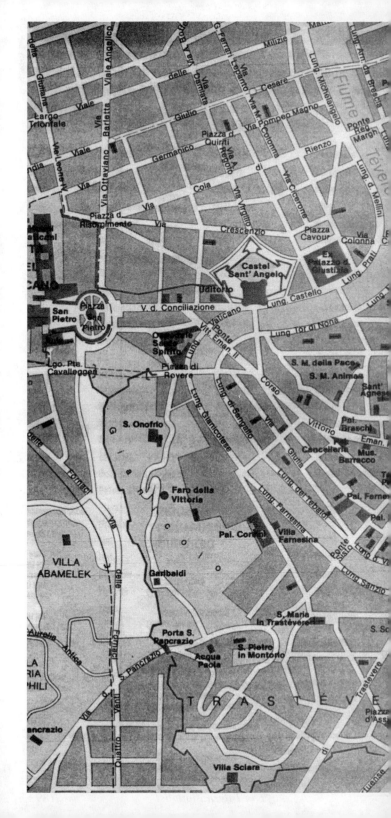

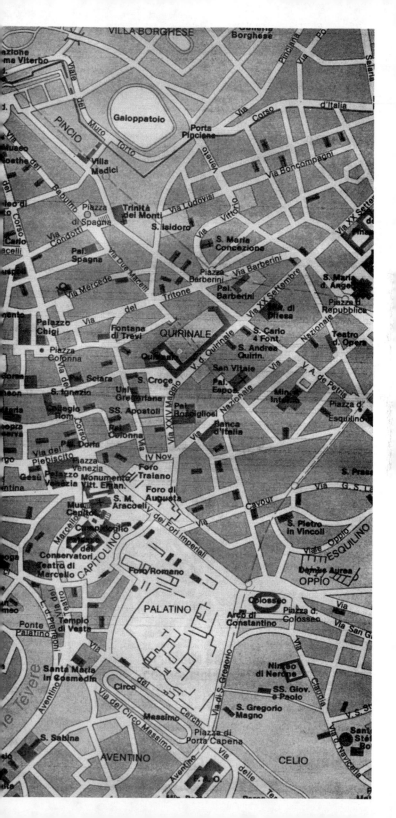

The Internationalist®

International Business and Travel

You may order any of the following titles from your favorite bookstore. Or you may contact The Internationalist at 96 Walter Street, Boston, MA 02131 USA.

The Top 10 Guide to Paris
ISBN: 1-891382-04-7 $14.95
The Top 10 Guide to London
ISBN: 1-891382-25-X $14.95
The Top 10 Guide to Rome
ISBN: 1-891382-20-9 $14.95
The Top 10 Guide to Florence
ISBN: 1-891382-05-5 $14.95
The Top 10 Guide to Beijing
ISBN: 1-891382-06-3 $14.95
The Top 10 Guide to New York City
ISBN: 1-891382-21-7 $14.95
The Top 10 Guide to Los Angeles
ISBN: 1-891382-23-3 $14.95
The Top 10 Guide to Hong Kong
ISBN: 1-891382-07-1 $14.95
The Top 10 Guide to Tokyo
ISBN: 1-891382-08-X $14.95
The Top 10 Guide to Singapore
ISBN: 1-891382-09-8 $14.95
The Top 10 Guide to San Francisco
ISBN: 1-891382-24-1 $14.95
The Top 10 Guide to Orlando-Disney World
ISBN: 1-891382-22-5 $14.95
The Top 10 Guide to Milan
ISBN: 1-891382-26-8 $14.95
The Top 10 Guide to Rio de Janeiro
ISBN: 1-891382-28-4 $14.95

e-mail: publisher@internationalist.com
web site: http://www.internationalist.com